C. J. (Charles John) Ellicott, Edward Harold Browne

The Inspiration of Holy Scripture

Being an Essay

C. J. (Charles John) Ellicott, Edward Harold Browne

The Inspiration of Holy Scripture
Being an Essay

ISBN/EAN: 9783337183530

Printed in Europe, USA, Canada, Australia, Japan

Cover: Foto ©ninafisch / pixelio.de

More available books at **www.hansebooks.com**

THE
INSPIRATION OF HOLY SCRIPTURE:

BEING

AN ESSAY,

BY

RT. REV. EDWARD HAROLD BROWNE, D.D.,

AND

A PORTION OF AN ESSAY,

BY

RT. REV. CHAS. JOHN ELLICOTT, D.D.

PRINTED FOR THE PROTESTANT EPISCOPAL SOCIETY FOR THE PROMOTION OF EVANGELICAL KNOWLEDGE.

NEW YORK:
T. WHITTAKER,
2 BIBLE HOUSE.

1879.

[The following Essays were originally published in a series of Theological Essays entitled, "AIDS TO FAITH."

S. W. GREEN,
Printer,
16 and 18 Jacob Street,
New York.

INSPIRATION.

CONTENTS.

1. INTRODUCTION—All Spiritual enlightenment derived from the Divine Spirit; but is all derived in the same way?
2. A Divine and human element in all inspiration—How co-existing?
3. History of the question—Jewish opinions—Patristic opinions.
4. No argument against a high view to be deduced from the patristic belief in the inspiration of others besides the Apostles.
5. Middle ages—Mysticism.
6. The Reformation favorable to a very high esteem of Holy Scripture, but favorable also to freedom of thought.
7. Tendency of thought in Germany in the eighteenth century.
8. Deism passed from England, through France, to Germany—Doctrine of the English Deists.
9. Causes leading to the controversy on inspiration in the present day.
10. English writers of the present century and their theories.
11. Christian Evidence in a measure independent of theories of inspiration.
12. Definite theories not desirable.
13. Objections to inspiration closely connected with objections to miracles.
14. Origin of doubts about miracles.
15. Miracles not improbable, if there be a spiritual world connected more or less closely with the physical world, and a Personal Ruler of the world.
16. If miracles ever should occur, we should most naturally expect them to be connected with some special communication of God's will to man.
17. The common course taken by philosophical scepticism.
18. As to inspiration: we have first certain phenomena in the Bible, proving the existence of a human element—The manifestation of that human element most valuable in the matter of evidence—We have next certain phenomena manifesting a Divine element—(*a*) Prophecy—Question as to the existence of true predictive prophecy in the Old Testament—Objection—Nihil in scripto quod non prius in Scriptore—Objection replied to—Cases of Balaam and Caiaphas—(*b*) Types.
19. How far all this proves the special inspiration of the Old Testament—Coleridge's view considered.
20. Argument *à fortiori* for the inspiration of the New Testament—Mr. Maurice's question replied to.
21. Mr. Morell's theory of the intuitional consciousness considered.
22. Latitude of opinion on some points may be allowable.
23. The Scriptures an *infallible* depository of *religious* truth.
24. Question concerning physical science.
25. Conclusion—Some trials of our faith ought not to stagger us—The proper condition of mind in the present day.

INSPIRATION.

1. As in the natural world wisdom and intelligence are among the signs of life in an intelligent being, so in the spiritual world a spiritual understanding follows on the possession of spiritual life. As the Divine Spirit gives life, so He inspires wisdom. Indeed all spiritual gifts flow equally from the same Spirit. St. Paul says that "there are diversities of gifts, but the same Spirit," who gives to one the word of wisdom, to another the word of knowledge, to another faith, to another miracles and gifts of healing, to another prophecy, to another divers kinds of tongues, to another the interpretation of tongues. So he describes the influence of that one and the self-same Spirit on the early disciples in the Church of Corinth. Are we to take this literally? Are we to believe that, whilst some had spiritual wisdom

and understanding—and that in larger or less degrees—others were enabled to work miracles, others to prophesy; that whilst to some there was only the common understanding of spiritual truths and mysteries, such as an enlightened mind among ourselves could penetrate, to others there was given an infallible knowledge of future events or of Divine truths otherwise unknown to man? Or, on the other hand, shall we think no more than this—that the Holy Spirit, who is the inspirer of all wisdom, by regenerating the heart, purifying the soul, exalting the affections, and quickening the intuitions of the mind, gives to some men more than to others an insight into things heavenly, and so enables them in all times and in all ages of the Church to be exponents of the Divine will?—that He reveals God and Christ in their inmost consciences, inspiring them with all high and holy thoughts, and that thus they can utter things which would be deep mysteries to other men, and which are, indeed, the oracles of God?

2. This is pretty much the question concerning inspiration so much agitated now. When we come to consider it, there can be no doubt but that we must admit a human and a Divine element. There is the mind of the

Prophet or Apostle to be enlightened, and the Holy Spirit, the inspirer or enlightener. The question will be, in what manner and in what proportion these two elements coexist. We may suppose the human mind perfectly passive, acting simply under a mechanical influence of the Holy Spirit, speaking or writing not its own thoughts or its own words, but only the thoughts and words of the Spirit of God. Or we may suppose the mind of the writer or speaker acting altogether freely, speaking entirely its own thoughts and words, but having derived from Divine communion and enlightenment a higher tone, having acquired a correcter judgment, and, from a deep spiritual insight, able to speak spiritual things such as the natural man receiveth not. These are the two extremes. The one is verbal inspiration, simple dictation, so that the lips of the Prophet and the pen of the Evangelist are but mechanical organs moved by the Spirit of God. The other is no more than an exaltation of the natural faculties by the influence of the same Spirit, such an exaltation as we must believe all wise and holy men to have received, an inspiration such as that by which a Hooker or a Butler wrote the works which bear their names. There are many intermediate steps between these two, but no one can exceed either of these extremes and yet call himself a Christian.

3. Many causes have brought this subject into controversy at present. It has, however, occupied the thoughts of thoughtful men, and has been debated and disputed on in earlier times; and a rapid glance at the history of the question may be a help to giving it its true place, and perhaps to finding its true solution.

The reverence which the ancient Jews felt for the Jewish Scriptures must have sprung from the highest theory of verbal inspiration. Their care to count every verse and letter in every book of the Old Testament, to retain every large or small letter, every letter above or below the line, their belief that a mystery lurked in every abnormal state of letter, jot, or tittle, cannot have resulted from any lower principle. Later Jews, like the Cabalists or Maimonides, may have become Pantheists, or Rationalists; but the more ancient have left us the clearest proof that they esteemed the Scriptures as the express word of God Himself. The well-known tradition amongst the Alexandrian Jews concerning the verbal agreement of all the LXX. translators, though working in seventy separate cells, looks the same way. There is considerable reason to believe that the distinction between the different books of Scripture—the Hagiographa being esteemed inferior to the Prophets, and the Prophets inferior to the law—was at least much magnified, if not wholly invented, by the later Jews. So far, however, as such a distinction and such difference of estimation existed at all, so far we must perhaps believe that there was a notion of something like degrees of inspiration.

The earlier Christian Fathers seem to have followed much the same course as their Jewish predecessors. Clemens Romanus calls the Holy Scriptures " the true words of the Holy Ghost" (c. 45). No definite theory of inspiration would be likely to be propounded ; but the general reverence for the words of Holy Writ, and the deep significance believed to exist underneath the letter, prove the belief in inspiration to have been very strong and universal. Justin Martyr and his Jewish opponent seem fully agreed in their appreciation of the Old Testament. "No Scripture can be opposed to any other Scripture." (' Dialog.' p. 289.) Irenæus saw in our Lord's promise to his Apostles—" He that heareth you, heareth Me" (Luke x. 16)—an assurance of their infallibility in the Gospel. "After the Lord's resurrection they were indued with the power of the Holy Ghost, and had perfect knowledge of the truth. He, therefore, who despises their teaching despises Christ and God." (Iren. iii. 1.) Still it may be fairly said that Irenæus, in his accounts of the composition of the Gospel, seems to combine a human element with the Divine. (See Iren. iii. 11.)

Tertullian embraced the Montanist belief, that Divine communications were made to man by means of a condition of trance or ecstasy. In this trance the prophet was supposed to lose all sense, like a Pythoness under the influence of the Divine afflatus. (c. Marcion. iv. 22.) This was the highest kind of inspiration. Yet he seems to have thought that the Apostles were at times allowed to speak their own words, and not the words of God, as where St. Paul (1 Cor. vii. 12) says, "To the rest speak I, not the Lord." ('De Monogam.' c. 3.)

The Alexandrian Fathers, Clement and Origen, though adopting somewhat of the Neo-Platonic views of the soul, as receiving an enlightenment by communion with the Divine Logos, appear to have held firmly the infallibility of every word of Scripture; and the

Mystical sense which they attach to the history and the language of the Old Testament seems to point even to verbal inspiration. (See Lumper, 'Historia Theologico-critica,' vol. 9. c. 4. § iii. art. 2.) Origen was, however, the first great Biblical critic: few things have tended more than Biblical criticism to modify the theory of verbal inspiration: and this appeared even in the patristic ages and among some of the most illustrious of the patristic writers. The critical labors of Chrysostom and Jerome, in the beginning of the fifth century, made them observe the apparent discrepancies in the account of the Evangelists, and other like difficulties in Holy Writ. Such observations led to a greater appreciation of the human element in the composition of Scripture. St. Chrysostom could see that some slight variations in the different narratives of the same event were no cause for anxiety or unbelief, but rather a proof that the Evangelists were independent witnesses. And St. Jerome could discern in the New Testament writers a dialect inferior to the purest Greek, and even at times a mixture of human passion in the language of the Apostles.* All this,

---

* Neander, 'History of Doctrines,' i. 280. (Bohn.)

however, these Fathers clearly held to be subjected and subordinate to the general Divine influence of the guiding and overruling Spirit.

4. No argument against a high doctrine of inspiration, as held by the Fathers, can be fairly deduced from the fact that they were disposed to admit the inspiration of other writings besides the Canonical Scriptures. Many of them knew the Old Testament only in the Greek translation, and were inclined to pay the same reverence to that which may have been due only to the Hebrew original. The writings of Clement and Hermas were at first received as canonical, though more careful inquiry excluded them from the Canon of the New Testament. This may be an argument against the critical accuracy of the Fathers, but is none against their belief in the inspiration of the Bible. Nor, again, are we warranted in thinking that they confounded natural enlightenment with spiritual inspiration, because some of them speak as if prophetic powers and supernatural illumination were vouchsafed to others besides the Apostles of Christ. There can be no question that the earlier Fathers believed in the continuation of the miraculous powers of the Apostolic age down to their own times, and hence they

looked themselves for a special illumination from the Holy Ghost. Yet, even so, they distinguished carefully between the gift of infallibility in things spiritual vouchsafed to the writers of the New Testament, and the gift of Divine illumination to themselves and their own contemporaries.*

5. The Church of the middle ages had, for the most part, a belief similar to that of the earlier Fathers. Visions, and dreams, and sensible illuminations were still expected. Miraculous powers and Divine inspiration were still believed to reside in the Church; but the Scriptures were not the less esteemed as specially, and in a sense distinct and peculiar, the lively oracles of God. Still the bold speculations of Abelard, in the twelfth century,

---

* Ignatius claims for himself that he knew the doctrines which he taught, not from man, but from the testimony of the Spirit ('ad Philadelph.' 7); but then he clearly distinguishes between himself and the Apostles. "I do not enjoin you as Peter and Paul; they were Apostles, I a condemned man." ('Ad. Eph.' 15.) And Tertullian, who took a peculiarly high view of the Divine illumination of the true Christian, says distinctly that "all the faithful have the Spirit of God, but all are not Apostles." "The Apostles have the Holy Spirit in a peculiar sense." ('De Exhortatione Castitatis,' 4.) See Westcott, 'Introd. to the Gospels,' pp. 386, 400.

reached the doctrine of inspiration as well as other deep questions of theology. The Prophets, as he taught, had sometimes the gift of prophecy and sometimes spoke from their own minds. The Apostles too were liable to error, as St. Peter on the question of circumcision, who was reproved by St. Paul.* Abelard's tendency was rationalistic. But here a very important phenomenon, not confined to the middle ages, but very apparent then, deserves our careful attention. In all ages of the Church we find frequent tendencies to mysticism. The desire for a kind of ecstatic vision of things Divine, of abstraction from the external world, and an absorbed contemplation of the Deity, is natural to enthusiastic temperaments, and is not uncommon in times of dogmatic controversy. The state so sought after seems to offer a refuge from the strife of tongues, from the din and noise and uncharitableness of the world and the Church without. Those who have taken this line, indulged in this spirit, have, of course, a firm belief in the communion of the Christian soul with the Spirit of God, and look for constant revela-

---

* 'Sic et Non.' Ed. Hencke, p. 10. See Neander, 'Hist. of Doctrine,' vol. ii. p. 492.

tions from the Divine to the human intelligence. The mystic is transported out of self, and aims at frequent supernatural communion with God. To such a person the condition of the devout soul is a condition of constant inspiration. It is very true that the Holy Spirit is ever present with the Church, ever dwells in the souls of Christians, is our teacher and guide in all things, is ever ready to enlighten our understandings, as well as to convert our hearts. But this truth of Scripture, pressed to the extent of mysticism, breaks down the boundary between the inspiration of Prophets or Apostles, and the enlightenment of the Christian soul. The genuine mystic is himself in a state of the highest inspiration. The intuitions of his spirit enable him to see things invisible. High doctrine concerning the Church is favorable enough to such a view of things. Belief in the infallibility of the existing Church, in its miraculous powers, and in frequent revelations to the higher Saints, looked all this way. Again, it is well known how mysticism tended to Pantheism. Striving after absorption in God, men learned to identify their own minds, more or less, with Deity. The Divine Spirit was believed to dwell in all human souls, and needed only to be stirred up within them. The inclination to look wholly within, neglect of the objective, cultivation only of the subjective—all this too readily takes a pantheistic direction. And so we find many sects of medieval mystics lapsing at length into pure Pantheism—a state of belief in which it is plain enough that anything like the Christian doctrine of the inspiration of the Scriptures is impossible, as it cannot be distinguished from the illumination of any devout mind, or from the inspirations of genius. This is a thing of great importance to observe, as it shows itself in subsequent ages of Church History. Mysticism and extreme spiritualism destroy any definite doctrine of the inspiration of Scripture, and they very readily glide into Pantheism.

6. The Reformation, of course, introduced much thought and controversy about Scripture. "The sufficiency of the Scriptures for salvation" became a Reformation watchword: Scripture, the written word of God,—not the unwritten record of the Church, Tradition. The natural inclination was to a very high esteem of the Bible, as the definite deposit of Christian truth, in contradistinction to the indefiniteness of the traditions of the Church, and of that teaching of the Holy Spirit ever pres-

ent with the Church, on which the Roman divines insisted. Nevertheless, the tendency of the Reformation was to boldness of thought and freedom of inquiry. Erasmus, the great forerunner of Luther, had from his critical investigations been led to a somewhat freer view of inspiration than had been common before him. He thought it unnecessary to attribute everything in the Apostles to miraculous teaching. Christ suffered the Apostles to err, and that too after the descent of the Paraclete, but not so as to endanger the faith.* Even Luther, the great master mind of the age, with his strong subjective tendency, and with his indomitable boldness, ventured to subject the books of the New Testament to the criterion of his own intuition. The teaching of St. Paul penetrated and convinced his soul; St. James seemed to contradict St. Paul; and his Epistle was rejected as an Epistle of straw. There is reason to believe that he afterwards regretted and retracted; but words once spo-

---

* Non est necesse ut quicquid fuit in Apostolis protinus ad miraculum vocemus. Passus est errare suos Christus, etiam post acceptum Paracletum, sed non usque ad fidei periculum.—Erasm. *Epistl.*, lib. ii. tom. iv. Edit. Basil.

ken reach far and wide, and can never be unsaid again.

The tendency of Calvin and the Calvinist reformers was less subjective and more scholastic than that of Luther and the Lutherans. Their distinct and definite system of doctrine, like that of their forerunners Augustine and Aquinas, naturally found a place for the plenary and even verbal inspiration of the Scriptures, so that some of the Swiss Confessions speak of simple dictation by the Holy Ghost. The Remonstrants or Arminians, on the other hand, were more disposed to Rationalism than the generality of the reformed; and writers, like Grotius and Episcopius, made clear distinctions between the Divine and the human element in the writers of the Old and New Testaments.*

The Socinians were, of course, the most rationalizing sect of those which early sprang from the Reformation, a fungus-growth, rather than one of the natural branches. At first, however, they took the same view as other Protestant writers of the authority of Holy Writ, only they were less sensitive about

* *E.g.* A Spiritu Sancto dictari *historias* non fuit opus. Satis fuit scriptorem memoriâ valere.—Grotius, *Vot. pro pace Eccles.*, tom. iii. p. 672. Lond. 1679.

difficulties and apparent discrepancies in Scripture, and more disposed to cut and square it so as to accord with what appeared to them to be reason and common-sense. This tendency more and more fully developed itself. The modern Unitarian is a genuine Rationalist, often little different from a Deist.

The mystical spirit, which had long been swelling up under the weight of the Medieval Church, sometimes wholly within it, sometimes bursting forth from the pressure, showed itself in many places and many forms, after the triumph of the Reformation. Its elevation of the subjective over the objective, of the inward life over the outward letter, led insensibly to a disregard of the Bible in comparison with the internal testimony and the intuition of the soul. The Anabaptists of Germany were of the coarsest class of mystics. Among the best have been the Quakers in this country. The leading principle of George Fox, their founder, was the doctrine of the Inward Light. This is the true principle of all knowledge of religion. The outward Word is chiefly valuable as it stirs up the Word within. The highest source of knowledge is this inward illumination. All outward forms, all outward tests, all creeds and confessions, are strictly forbidden. Even the Bible must be subordinated to the light of God within. It is evident that, on this principle, there can be no distinction between the inspiration of Prophets and Apostles and the inspiration of every devout soul. It is also observable how this theory produces results like those which spring from the Roman doctrine of tradition. The written Word of God is no longer the final court of appeal in controversies of doctrine. The Church of Rome finds an infallible interpreter in that Divine Spirit which ever dwells in and guides the Church. The mystic has an infallible interpreter in his own bosom, who not only opens his understanding that he may understand the Scriptures, but communicates directly and sensibly truth to the soul. It is also very deserving of remark, however painful it may be, that at one time the Quakers were rapidly hurrying into Rationalism, and even Socinianism—the coldest forms of unbelief—from the warm mysticism of their first founders.

7. To come nearer to our own times, the whole spirit of the last century in Germany was subjective. There seemed a reaction from the positive spirit of the seventeenth century, which has been called the middle age of the

Reformation. Pietism was the form taken by the religious revival, a form which was eminently subjective, and which partook much of the mystical. The philosophical spirit was of the same character. The very principle of illuminism (aufklärung) was, that there is in man's inmost consciousness an intuitional knowledge of truth. Its motto—"Wahr ist was klar ist," "that is true which is clear" —sufficiently indicates its character. Proceeding from such a ground, and raising Natural Religion to the rank of a Revelation, Töllner, the disciple of Wolff, reduced Scripture to the level of a natural light.* At the same time, the Pietists used the Bible, not so much to be the source of truth and the fountain of faith, as for a book of devotion and to raise pious emotions.† In both ways there was a move towards the confounding of the light of Nature with the light of Revelation, of the light of the Spirit in the devout or illuminated soul with the light which had been specially vouchsafed to Prophets and Apostles for communicating God's truth to the world.

8. In the latter half of the eighteenth cen-

---

* See Kahnis, 'Hist. of German Protestantism,' English Translation, by Meyer, p. 116.
† Ib., pp. 100, 116.

tury, the Deism which had been troubling England had passed through the alembic of French scepticism, and now settled down in a shower of Rationalism on Germany. The Rationalism of Paulus, the Pantheism of Hegel, the historical myth of Strauss, derive their pedigree from the writings of Lord Herbert of Cherbury, Toland, Tindall, and other English Deists of the seventeenth and early eighteenth centuries, through the school of Rousseau and Voltaire.* The special principle of Lord Herbert and his followers, the Deists, was that there were several positive religions— Christianity, Judaism, Mohammedanism, etc. In the main all these are the same. The *general* religion is at the bottom of all of them, *i.e.*, the Religion of Nature, a religion founded in the natural perception of truth, the intuitional consciousness of the human mind. Positive religions may be very good for practical purposes; but all that is positive in them is evil, or at the best worthless; the valuable part being that which they hold in common of the general religion. It was this principle which passed through the various forms of French infidelity, German Rationalism and Panthe-

* See Kahnis as above, p. 31, etc. McCaul's 'Rationalism and Deistic Infidelity,' passim.

ism, and which has been brought back to us, as the highest result of modern discoveries in science and mental philosophy. How it was calculated to act upon the theory of inspiration, and to unsettle it even with those who had not become either Rationalists or Deists, it is needless to remark. Where a shadow of infidelity is obscuring the light, many, who are not wholly under its darkness, will yet pass through the penumbra that surrounds it. Even the apologist in the last century, from the wish to take positions which were impregnable, surrendered, at least for argument's sake, the higher ground of their forerunners in the faith. And, in the like manner, among the German divines, who still held Christian and orthodox opinions, there was a tendency to depart from the higher doctrine of inspiration held by the Church and the Reformers; to speak of degrees of inspiration, of fallibility in things earthly, of a Divine influence elevating the mental faculties of the sacred writers; not simply to ascribe all to the direct teaching of the Spirit of God.*

9. Distinct theories of inspiration were in old times seldom propounded, even where

---

* See Kahnis, pp. 116, 117.

some attention was directed to the question. Definite controversies upon it scarcely arose. The present century has been rife in both; and they have prevailed not a little among ourselves. Several causes have contributed to call them forth. First, and chiefly, the spread of rationalizing speculations, and the consequent unsettling of faith.* Next, the greater attention which has been paid to the criticism of the Bible, and especially of the New Testament, has exposed to view some of the difficulties concerning the origin of the books of the Bible, concerning the historical accuracy of some statements, concerning the slight apparent variations in the testimony of the Evangelists. In ordinary historians these would puzzle no one. The strictest integrity is compatible with slight inaccuracy or divergence of testimony; but if all was the work of God's Holy Spirit, speaking through human agents, the least discrepancy is formidable. Hence the

---

* It is important to observe, that this was first in *time* as well as in importance. Dr. McCaul has shown clearly ('Rationalism and Deistic Infidelity') that the spread of unbelieving opinions in Germany was first, the criticism came afterwards. Faith in Revelation was shaken by Deism and Rationalism, and then the unfriendly criticism was brought to bear upon the records of Christianity.

human element has been thought more of among modern critics, and by some has been elevated above the Divine. Thirdly, the rapid discoveries of modern science have been supposed to contradict the records of the Old Testament Scriptures; and, in order to account for such a contradiction, efforts have been made to interpret anew the words of Moses; and, where these have proved unsatisfactory, many have more or less believed that the writers of the historical books were merely chroniclers of historical events or collectors of ancient records, the providence of God having watched over the preservation of such records, but the Spirit of God having in no sense dictated them. Still freer views have been propounded; but this may suffice as the expression of the thoughts of serious men.

10. One of the first among ourselves to put forth a bold theory of inspiration was Coleridge. His 'Confessions of an Enquiring Spirit' was indeed not published till after his death; but the tone of many former writings is much the same. In the posthumous work just mentioned he unfolds his theory pretty freely. Of the Bible he speaks as a library of infinite value, as that which must have a Divine Spirit in it, from its appeal to all the

hidden springs of feeling in our hearts. "In short," he writes, "whatever *finds* me bears witness that it has proceeded from a Holy Spirit." (Letter i.) "In the Bible there is more that finds me than I have experienced in all other books put together; the words of the Bible find me at greater depths of my being; and whatever finds me brings with it an irresistible evidence of its having proceeded from the Holy Spirit." (Letter ii.) But then he protests against "the doctrine which requires me to believe that not only what finds me, but all that exists in the sacred volume, and which I am bound to find therein, was not only inspired by, that is, composed by men under the actuating influence of, the Holy Spirit, but likewise dictated by an Infallible Intelligence; that the writers, each and all, were divinely informed, as well as inspired." The very essence of this "doctrine is this, that one and the same Intelligence is speaking in the unity of a person, which unity is no more broken by the diversity of the pipes through which it makes itself audible, than is a tune by the different instruments on which it is played by a consummate musician equally perfect in all. One instrument may be more capacious than another, but as far as its compass extends, and in what it sounds forth, it will be true to the conception of the master." Such a doctrine, he conceives, must imply infallibility in physical science and in everything else as much as in faith, in things natural no less than in spiritual. He expresses a full belief "that the word of the Lord came to Samuel, to Isaiah, to others, and that the words which gave utterance to the same are faithfully recorded." But for the recording he does not think that there was need of any supernatural working, except in such cases as those in which God not only utters certain express words to a prophet, but also enjoins him to record them. In the latter case he accepts them "as supernaturally communicated and their recording as executed under special guidance." The arguments of Coleridge are calculated rather to pull down than to build up. He brings many reasons against a rigid mechanical theory, against a belief that the Bible is simply the voice of God's Holy Spirit uttered through different organs or instruments; but he does not fix any limit, he does not say how far he admits Divine teaching or inspiration to extend, nor does he apparently draw any line of distinction between the inspiration of Holy men of old and the spiritual and providential direction of enlightened men in every age and nation.

Wherever Coleridge has trodden Mr. Maurice follows him; not that he is a servile imitator, but he is a zealous disciple, and one who generally outdoes his master. In his 'Theological Essays' he begins to speak of the inspiration of poets and prophets among the Greeks; he speaks again of the quickening and informing spirit, to which all good men ascribe their own teaching and enlightenment; he quotes the language of our Liturgy as ascribing to "God's holy inspiration" the power of "thinking those things that be good;" and then he asks the question, "Ought we in our sermons to say, 'Brethren, we beseech you not to suppose the inspiration of Scripture to at all resemble that for which we have been praying; they are generically and essentially unlike; it is blasphemous to connect them in our minds; the Church is very guilty for having suggested the association'?" Proceeding in this course he naturally arrives at the conclusion that all which is good and beautiful comes from the inspiration of the Spirit of God, and that the sacred words of Scripture came in the same manner from the same Spirit. (See Essay xiii.) In some of his writings, especially in his work on ' Sacrifices,' he appears to have carried his disbelief of a more *special* inspiration of Holy Scripture to a greater length than in his ' Theological Essays,' as where God's tempting of Abraham to slay his son is attributed to a horrible thought coming over him and haunting him.

A very able and interesting writer on the same side of the same subject is Mr. Morell in his ' Philosophy of Religion.' The work is one of considerable acuteness and philosophical power. The writer's theory of inspiration is based on his theory of the human mind. The different powers of consciousness he classes thus:

Powers of Consciousness	..to which correspond..	Emotions.
1. The Sensational	" "	The Instincts.
2. The Perceptive	" "	The Animal Passions.
3. The Logical	" "	Relational Emotions.
4. The Intuitional	" "	Æsthetic, Moral, and Religious Emotions.

Now, the intuitional consciousness, he contends, is that which alone is properly susceptible of religious impressions and religious truths. Revelation he considers to involve an immediate intuition of Divine realities. All revelation implies an intelligible object presented, and a given power of recipiency in the subject, which power is lodged in the intuitional consciousness. In distinguishing revelation and inspiration, he defines "revelation, in the Christian sense, as that act of the Divine power by which God presents the realities of the spiritual world immediately to the human mind, while inspiration denotes that especial influence wrought upon the faculties of the subject, by virtue of which he is able to grasp these realities in their perfect fulness and integrity" (p. 150). "God made a revelation of Himself to the world in Jesus Christ; but it was the inspiration of the Apostles, which enabled them clearly to discern it."

Mr. Morell argues that "the canonicity of the New Testament Scriptures was decided upon solely on the ground of their presenting to the whole Church clear statements of *Apostolical* Christianity. The idea of their being written by any special command of God, or verbal dictation of the Spirit, was an idea altogether foreign to the primitive Christians" (p. 165). "The proper idea of inspiration, as applied to the Holy Scriptures, does not include either miraculous powers, verbal dictation, or any distinct commission from God." (*Ib.*) On the contrary, it consists "in the impartation of clear intuitions of moral and spiritual truth to the mind by extraordinary means. According to this view of the case, inspiration, *as an internal phenomenon*, is perfectly consistent with the natural laws of the human mind—it is a higher kind of potency, which every man to a certain degree possesses" (p. 166). This view, he thinks, " gives full consistency to the *progressive* character of Scripture morality" (p. 167). " It gives a satisfactory explanation of the minor discrepancies to be found in the sacred writers" (p. 170), whether those discrepancies be between Scripture and science, or in statements of facts, or in reasoning. In every case in which the moral nature is highly purified, and so a harmony of the spiritual being with the mind of God produced, a removal of all outward disturbances from the heart, " what," he asks, " is to prevent or disturb the immediate intuition of Divine things ? ' Blessed are the pure in heart, for they shall *see* God ' " (p. 186).

It is clear that this theory makes great purity of heart, or high sanctification, equivalent to, or the unfailing instrument of, inspiration. If one man is a better Christian than another, and so has a purer heart, he must be more inspired than the other. Hence, if a man of modern times could be found of a higher religious tone and character than an Apostle, he would have a higher intuition of Divine things, and therefore would know Christian truth more infallibly. Moreover, it appears that the value of the Scriptures consists, not in their proceeding from any direct command of God, or from any infallible guidance of His Spirit, but in their embodying the teaching and experience of men whose hearts were elevated, and so their understandings enlightened; to this it being added, in the case of the New Testament, that the writers were such as were specially qualified to represent the Apostolical Church, and so to transmit its spirit and teaching to us.

A writer of less ability, but more boldness, Mr. MacNaught of Liverpool, has carried the same theory to its furthest limits. He defines inspiration to be "that action of the Divine Spirit by which, apart from any idea of infallibility, all that is good in man, beast, or matter is originated and sustained" (p. 136, Second Edition). He denies all distinction between genius and inspiration. He doubts not that "David, Solomon, Isaiah, or Paul would have spoken of everything, which may with propriety be called a work of genius, or of cleverness, or of holiness," as "works of the

Spirit of God, written by Divine inspiration" (p. 132).

11. The historical sketch thus rapidly given seems to show that there have always been some slight differences of tone and opinion touching this important question, but that these differences have never so markedly come out as in the nineteenth century. The subject at present causes great anxiety, and not without reason. Many feel that, if they must give up a high doctrine of inspiration, they give up Christianity; and yet they think that a high doctrine is scarcely tenable. Such a feeling is not unnatural, and yet it is not wholly true. All the history, and even all the great doctrines of the Gosepl, might be capable of proof, and so deserving of credence, though we were obliged to adopt almost the lowest of the modern theories of inspiration. For instance, all, or almost all, the arguments of Butler, Paley, Lardner, and other like authors, are independent of the question, "What is the nature and degree of Spiritual inspiration?" Paley, for instance, undertakes to prove the truth of Christ's resurrection and of the Gospel history, and thence the truth of the doctrines which Christ taught to the world. But this he argues out, for the most part, on prin-

ciples of common historical evidence. He treats the Apostles as twelve common men, of common honesty and common intelligence. If they could not have been deceived, and had no motive to deceive the world, then surely we must accept their testimony as true. But if their testimony is true, Jesus Christ must have lived, and taught, and worked miracles, and risen from the dead, and so in Him we have an accredited witness sent from God. His teaching, therefore, must have been the truth; and if we have good grounds for believing that His disciples carefully treasured up His teaching, and faithfully handed it on to us, we have then in the New Testament an unquestionable record of the will and of the truth of God. Even if the Apostles and Evangelists had no special inspiration, yet, if we admit their care and fidelity, we may trust to their testimony, and so accept their teaching as true.

So, then, even if we were driven to take the lowest view of inspiration, we are not bound to give up our faith. External evidence must almost of necessity begin by taking low ground. It must treat nothing as certain until it is proved. It must not, therefore, even presume that witnesses are honest till it has found reason to think them so ; and, of course, it cannot treat them as inspired till it meets with something which compels an acknowledgment of their inspiration. This is taking the extremest case, one in which we altogether doubt the inspiration of the Apostles. *A fortiori*, we need not throw away all faith, if we should be led to think that some books of the Old Testament are only historical records, collected by Jewish antiquarians, and bound up with the writings of prophets, as venerable and valuable memorials of the peculiar people of God. All this might be, and yet God may have spoken by holy men of old, and afterwards more fully by His Son.

Some Christian controversialists, who take high ground themselves, write as if they thought that Christianity was not worth defending, unless it was defended exactly on their principles. The minds of the young more especially are sometimes greatly endangered by this means. The defender of the Gospel may be but an indifferent reasoner. He fails to make his ground sure and strong. His reader finds more forcible, at least more specious, arguments elsewhere. He thinks the advocate he rested on defeated, his arguments answered and upset, and Christianity itself seems lost. Now, we may surely begin by saying, that the question of inspiration is, within certain limits, a question *internal* to Christianity. No doubt, it may materially affect the evidences of Christianity; but the questions of verbal inspiration, mechanical inspiration, dynamical inspiration, and the like, are all questions on which persons believing in the Gospel may differ. There is a degree of latitude which must be fatal to faith; but within certain limits men may differ, and yet believe. We shall be wise to take safe ground ourselves, and to bear as charitably as we can with those who may take either higher or lower. Only it cannot be concealed that the temper of mind which disposes to a very low doctrine of inspiration is one that may not improbably lead in the end to the rejection of many religious truths—to scepticism, if not to unbelief.

12. It seems pretty generally agreed among thoughtful men at present, that definite theories of inspiration are doubtful and dangerous.

The existence of a human element, and the existence of a Divine element, are generally acknowledged; but the exact relation of the one to the other it may be difficult to define.

Yet some thoughts may aid us to an approximation to the truth, perhaps sufficiently clear for practical purposes.

13. In the first place, then, let us consider for a moment what is the real principle which seems to actuate those writers and thinkers, of the present day especially, who endeavor to root out all distinction between the inspiration of the Apostles and Prophets, and the ordinary illumination of good and wise men. Is it not that morbid shrinking from a belief in anything miraculous in religious history, now so commonly prevalent? that fear to admit the possibility that the Creator of the universe should ever specially interfere with the universe which He has created? There can be no question but that that inspiration of Holy Scripture in which the Church has generally believed is of the nature of a miracle; and so its rejection follows upon the rejection of miracles in general. Many marvellous things exist in nature, things at least as marvellous as any miracles recorded in Scripture. It is marvellous that the worlds should have come into being, and should all be under the government of the strictest laws and the most undeviating rules—that life should exist at all—that new life should be constantly bursting

forth—that eyes should open curiously formed to see, and ears curiously constructed to hear; —all this, and much beside, is as marvellous as the suspension of a natural law, as the restoring life to the body from which it had gone forth, as the giving sight to the blind, or hearing to the deaf. But the latter startles us into conviction that some living personal being of creative power has newly put forth his strength; the former state of things is so general, uniform, and constantly recurring, that we can go on as usual without much thinking of it, call it nature, or perhaps Deity, or any other abstract generality, and so rest satisfied.

14. Without doubt we witness in the universe the constant prevalence of general laws, and the regulation of all things by them. In proportion to this general constancy is our natural expectation that it will continue. And, moreover, even though we may be led to believe that the whole must have been framed, and that the laws must have been given by a creative intelligence; still the uniform operation of those laws disposes us to doubt the probability that they will ever be interfered with by the hand that first ordered them. This doubt is strengthened by the belief that the wisdom, which first gave being to an universe,

could never have wrought so imperfectly as that its active interference should afterwards be needed, to remedy defects or to repair the machinery. And all this might perhaps be probable enough, if we could see but a natural creation, and if there were no moral and rational creation too. But suppose it to be true, that there is in the physical universe, and more or less connected with matter and the laws of matter, a multitude of intelligent, rational, moral, and accountable beings; some more powerful than others; some, the angels, wholly good; some, the evil angels, wholly bad; some of a mixed character, like man; all capable, more or less, of communication with each other—those indeed of mixed character closely connected with matter, joined to material bodies, whilst the more powerful intelligences, good and evil, are freer and more independent of mere physical influences: suppose, too, that there is one great Intellect, one Sovereign Mind, who made all, and who governs all; with premises like these, where is the improbability that there should be occasional interferences with natural laws? Life does not exist at all without producing some interference with the mere laws of matter and motion. Where intelligent beings exist capable of acting on material substances, they ever do mould those material substances to their will, and make the laws of nature serve them. If created intelligences superior to man have any power to act through material instruments, we should expect that they could only act, as man does, by taking advantage of the laws by which matter is guided, and so controlling one law by bringing a more powerful law to bear upon it. Even of the providence of the Supreme Being, if that providence be continually at work, controlling the moral and intellectual, and upholding the material creation, it is most probable that such providential agency would be exercised in overruling and directing natural causes and laws rather than in displacing or superseding them. But there certainly seems no *à priori* improbability that the Creator should be also the Ruler of the universe; that where the creation is moral and intelligent, He should rule and interfere as He might not where it was simply material or animal; that, where moral, personal beings were acting upon one another, striving to benefit, and striving to ruin one another, He too at times should be at hand, to punish or to protect. And so the doctrine of a special providence seems only consistent with the belief in a personal God. But the step from thence to a belief in miracles is no great stride. For, if the great personal Creator rules and guides and interferes in the affairs of His creation, though he would be likeliest to do so commonly by mere guidance of natural laws, yet, if there were need or occasion for it, it must be quite as easy for Him to interfere by the entire suspension of those laws, or by a temporary alteration of them.*

15. Indeed it is hard to see how miracles should appear either impossible or improbable; but either on the theory that what we see commonly we must see always, or else on the theory that there is no personal providence of God. And, in short, is it not true, that the natural tendency of those who try to get rid of miracle and special inspiration is to the resolving of providence into law, and of God into

* Of course, if the Professor Baden Powell's theory be true, that the physical and the spiritual worlds are so separate that they can never come in contact, then all this is impossible. But then all creation is impossible. The spiritual could never have created the material. Indeed, the union of soul and body must be impossible; at all events, all religious knowledge must be impossible. It can be founded on no evidence, and can result only from certain convictions of the mind, wholly incapable of being tested as to their truth.

simple intelligence? We are all well aware that we see the government of law, not only in the physical, but even in the intellectual world; and there are those, who, from observing this, have been led to a belief in law, and nothing but law. God with them is but law; and providential or moral government gives place to mere necessity. Of course, this is simple Atheism, and involves all the difficulties, as well as all the miseries, of Atheism. And yet, surely it is more consistent and logical than the system, which does not deny the wisdom that seems to have planned and still seems to order all things, but which yet shrinks from acknowledging the distinct, individual personality of the Creator, His personal presence to all the universe which He has created, His superintending providence over it, and His active interference in it. Unquestionably this latter is the doctrine of the Hebrew Bible, and that which Jesus Christ taught in the Sermon on the Mount. But philosophic religion talks to us of a general principle of intelligence diffused throughout all things, moving, and breathing in, and animating all beings. Now this general principle of intelligence sounds philosophical enough; but how can it be reconciled with what Englishmen call common-sense? What, on principles of common reason, can be meant by intelligence where there is no intellect, or a great principle of mind where there is no personal mind at all? We know what is meant by the intelligence of a man, or the intelligence of a beast—intelligence being the power of perceiving, understanding, and reasoning predicable of the mind of that man or that beast. In like manner we can understand, that if there be one great infinite mind, then infinite intelligence may be predicable of that infinite mind. But to say that there is any general principle of intelligence separable and distinguishable from any particular mind, is surely to palter with us in a double sense. We can no more appreciate intelligence as separated from the intellect of which it is a quality or attribute, than we can understand agency without an agent, potency without a power, sight without a seer, thought without a thinker, or life without that which lives. In short, may we not demur altogether to mere abstractions, except as they may exist in the mind, or in systems of philosophy? And so, is not the conclusion inevitable, that our real alternative lies between a mere Stoical law, a Buddhist Kharma, blind and inexorable, working in matter, it is useless to inquire whence or how—between this and a belief in a God, personal, present, Maker, Ruler, Guider of all things, and of all men?

16. Give us this, as the Bible gives Him to us: and though we should never expect Him to be perpetually setting aside the laws which He has made for the universe, yet we need not —rather we cannot—believe, that He should be so inevitably fettered by them, as that He should not continually guide them for the good of His intelligent and moral creatures—guide them as in a less degree those creatures themselves can guide them, or that, when He may see fit, He should not suspend, or even for a season alter them. And if this latter contingency should ever take place, we should naturally expect that it would be never so probable as when it was His pleasure to communicate to rational beings some special revelation of His will, and to teach them concerning Himself what they might not be able to learn from mere natural phenomena.

Can there be any inconsistency in such a putting aside of the veil of nature, and giving man a somewhat clearer vision of God? Doubtless, other causes are possible. God might be pleased, instead of making any objective communications to mankind, to breathe silently into each individual spirit, and to teach separately each one of His will and of Himself. But no one has a right to say that such must be God's plan of action—that such only is consistent with Divine wisdom, or human capacity, or philosophical theology. If God be not the mere pervading intelligence, which informs the universe, but which can exert itself only through the medium of things in the universe ; if, on the contrary, He is a personal, present ruler and guide, there can be no inconsistency in the belief that He may at times let Himself be heard by those who can hear Him—in other and clearer tones than the voices of mere natural phenomena, or even of the intuitional consciousness.

17. Now, the common course which we see philosophic scepticism taking at present is this : First, there is a doubt about miracles, then about special inspiration. To build our faith in any degree on miracles is unwise. Inspiration is wholly a question of degree. One man has by the teaching or breathing of God's Spirit greater insight into spiritual truth than another. The Apostles, doubtless, had an unusual brightness of such vision, and so we may truly call their writings inspired ; but the difference between their inspiration and that

of St. Augustine, or even of Plato, is but a difference of degree. Next comes a doubt or a denial of the existence of personal spiritual beings. The devil, Satan, wicked spirits are but names for a general evil principle, which we cannot but see and feel influencing and pervading ourselves and all things around us. Angels are soon placed in the same category; and the last step of all reduces God Himself to a principle of intelligence, if it does not go yet farther, and make Him but a law.

But in all honesty, is there a middle course? Does not the Bible at all events—Old Testament and New alike—speak of a present, personal God, of a multitude of personal spiritual beings—some good and others evil—working around us and within us, of miracles wrought by teachers sent from God, of predictions uttered before the event, of holy men of old moved by the Spirit of God to speak things, which could be known to none but God Himself? It is quite impossible to get rid of all this, and to retain the Bible as in any proper sense true. Let it be said, that good men who wrote books of the Bible were good men, but spoke according to the prejudices of their times. They believed in prophecies and miracles, and evil spirits, and so spoke of them.

Their inspiration quickened their intuitions, but it did not make them infallible, and so in these matters they may have erred. But, if Christianity be Christianity, and not a system of mere morals and philosophy, there was One Man, who was so much more than man, that if we disbelieve Him, we make God Himself a liar. And may we not ask, if His discourses be not so unfaithfully handed down to us that we might as well or better not have them at all, whether He did not perpetually appeal to miracles, whether He did not continually quote prophecies as fulfilled or soon to be fulfilled, whether He did not speak much of angels and devils, whether He did not in the most signal manner promise to His disciples the guidance and teaching of His Holy Spirit, to bring to their remembrance all that He had said to them, and to lead them into all truth? Is it possible to reject all this without rejecting Christ?

18. And so much of miracles and inspiration generally. Now let us take a few facts, and see what they seem to teach us. We have a number of different books written in different styles, indicating the different characters of the writers. At times, too, there appear slight diversities of statements in trifling matters of detail. Here we mark a human element. If

God spoke, it is plain that He spoke through man ; if God inspired, He inspired man. Even the Gospel *miracles* were often worked with some instrumental means ; no wonder, then, that when God would teach men, He would teach through human agency. And the difference of style—perhaps the slight discrepancies in statements — seem to satisfy us that some portions at least of the Bible were not simply dictated by God to man ; there was not what is called mere mechanical or organic inspiration ; God did not simply speak God's words, using as a mere machine man's lips to speak them with. Of course, we must not forget the benefit we derive from these differences between writers of the same narrative. The apparent or trifling discrepancies in the statements of the different Evangelists, for instance, convince us that they were independent witnesses, and that the whole story did not arise from some well-concerted plan to deceive the world : the homely and even barbarous style of some of the writers proves to us that they were really fishermen, and not philosophers ; and so we have a convincing evidence that the deepest system of theology, and the noblest code of ethics ever propounded—the one stirring the depths of the whole human heart, the other guiding all human life—came, not from the profound speculations of the wisest of mankind, but either from God Himself, or else from a source more inexplicable and impossible ; from the poor, the narrow-minded, and the untaught. But whilst we see the benefit of all this, and admire the wisdom which so ordered it, we learn from it that there must have been a human element in Scripture ; that God may, nay must, have spoken, but that He dealt His own common dealing with us—that is, He used earthly instruments for giving heavenly blessings, human means for communicating Divine truth.

Now, let us look the other way. Scripture is not a mere system of theology, nor is it a mere historical record. If it were either or both of these, and nothing more, of course we could believe that nothing might be needed, beyond the quickening of the intuitional consciousness, to enable men to conceive its truths and to communicate them to others. There is, however, as has been already noticed, a distinctly miraculous element in it ; and here, if we admit its existence, we cannot fail to see the working of a present, personal God. Take away the miraculous element, and we may easily get into any kind of philosophical abstraction. Admit it, and we are brought back again into the intelligible region of common, plain sense.

If anything in the world can be supernatural or miraculous, it surely must be the infallible foreknowledge of future events. No elevation of the intuitional consciousness can account for such foreknowledge. None can certainly foretell the future, but one who can certainly guide the future. Do we, then, admit that any of the prophets in the Old Testament were enabled to foretell coming events, the events of the Gospel history in particular? Some modern writers go so far as to deny this *in toto*. According to them every prophecy of the Old Testament concerned, primarily at least, contemporaneous history, or history so nearly contemporaneous, that it required only common foresight and " old experience" to look into it. Burke early shadowed forth the French Revolution: Isaiah, on the same principle, could forewarn Israel of its dangers, threaten sinners with punishment, and promise protection to penitents. Of course, we can understand such a view; but can we admit it and not reject Christianity? And let us remember that, in arguing on the nature of inspiration, we are not arguing in proof of

Christianity; but that, admitting the truth of Christianity, we are inquiring into somewhat which, as has been already observed, is really internal to Christianity. Most Christians are ready to believe that the passages of the Old Testament to which our Lord and his Apostles appealed, as proofs of His Divine mission and of the truth of their teaching, were really predictions, and not guesses. This is not the place to enter at length into such a question. But, if we just think of what Jacob said of Shiloh—Moses, of a prophet like himself—David and others, of a great Son of David—Isaiah, in his ninth and fifty-third chapters, of a Child born, a Son given, called Mighty God, Eternal Father, Prince of Peace, and of a righteous Servant, on whom the LORD should lay the iniquity of us all—Daniel, of Messiah the Prince, cut off, but not for Himself, and of one like a Son of Man, to whom a kingdom is given by the Ancient of days, an everlasting kingdom, a dominion that shall not pass away—Haggai, of the glory of the second temple, so much surpassing that of the first—Malachi, of the forerunner of the Messiah—and many prophecies of like kind; we shall feel that the burden of proof must lie with those who deny, not with those who believe.

that there were prophets, who bore witness to the coming of the Christ centuries before His birth.* We may remember that these predictions have been preserved to us both in the original Hebrew, and in translations made from the Hebrew before the birth of Christ, made not by Christians, but by Jews—that the more ancient Jews did undeniably interpret these prophecies, as pointing forward to a prince who should be sent from heaven to save their own nation, and to bless other nations in them. Comparatively modern Jews have explained some of these prophecies away, because they too manifestly favor the Christians; but even so, they continue to believe that the Scriptures foretold a Messiah. Moreover, we have the clearest testimonies from Jews and Gentiles alike (Jews and Gentiles

---

* It matters little to this argument whether all the books of the Old Testament were written by those whose names they bear; whether, for instance, the last chapters of Isaiah were Isaiah's or some other's; whether the book of Daniel was written at the time of the captivity, or not collected till some centuries later. It is certain they were all written before Christ; and if in them there be found prophecies of the Messiah, prophecies, be they many or few, like precious stones imbedded in a rock; we have then the phenomenon existing, and we have to explain how it came. ' Idoneum, opinor, testimonium divinitatis veritas divinationis.' (Tert. *Apolog.* c. 20.)

who never became Christians, and so are independent witnesses) that in the East generally, *Oriente toto*, and especially among the Israelites themselves, there had prevailed an ancient and constant persuasion that by Divine appointment a Deliverer was to arise out of Judea, who should have dominion ; and, moreover, that he was impatiently expected in the reigns of the early emperors of Rome. Jews, who have lived since those times, have confessed that the period presignified is apparently past. Now, it is quite certain that the most remarkable and most influential religious teacher that ever lived in any nation upon earth did arise and live in Judea, at the time so marked and agreed on. It is undoubted that He declared the predictions in question to have pointed to Him. His followers have always claimed them as fulfilled in Him. Of all religious revolutions, nay, of all revolutions, moral, spiritual, social, or political, ever produced in the world, He has produced the greatest, the most influential, the most extensive. As Christians, we, of course, believe that He was the Christ ; and we are justified in urging on the Jews such considerations as the above, in proof that their own cherished Scriptures pointed to Him.

Now, if the prophets really did centuries before foresee an event, most unlikely, but which we have witnessed as true, they must have had something more than the inspiration of genius, or than the exalting of their intuitional consciousness. For, whatever degree of insight into the truth of things spiritual we may attribute to such intuitional consciousness, and whatever communion it may give with the mind of God, it can hardly be said to make us partakers of God's omniscience, or to endue us with His powers of foresight.

One of the favorite modes of evading such conclusions as this, and so one of the favorite positions of the low inspirationists is, that *Nihilin scripto quod non prius inscriptore;* a man can speak nothing but what he thinks. In a sense this is true enough ; and, as a general rule, we may suppose the holy men of old, who spake as they were moved by the Holy Ghost, to have been first gifted with the knowledge of the future, and then moved to communicate that knowledge to others. But still, if there be an overruling and over-guiding Providence as well as an informing and inspiring Spirit, may not a man be guided to speak unconsciously words of deep import? We see this in the Old Testament in the case of Balaam. If the history of him be not a false legend or a mere myth, the Almighty told him that he was to speak to Balak that word which was put into his mouth. His will was quite the other way. He willed to curse Israel, and so to obtain from Balak the wages of unrighteousness; but his own will was overruled by the direct command of God. If Balaam prophesied, if he prophesied, as most Christians have believed, not only of the future fortunes of Israel, but of the future coming of Christ; it is certain that his extraordinary knowledge could not have been the result of his purity of heart qualifying him to see God, could not have come from the clearing away of those clouds of sin, and therefore of error, which darken the mental vision; for his heart was set upon covetousness, and he perished with the enemies of God. The same, or much the same, may be said of Caiaphas, who was altogether bent on evil, and yet of whom the Evangelist testifies that "being High Priest that year he prophesied." If miracles are impossible, of course, all this is impossible. But how miracles can be impossible, unless God is impossible, it seems that we have yet to learn.

Though, therefore, we may not generally

look for a work of the Spirit through the mere bodily organs of men, without an elevation of their souls ; we surely have no power to limit the operations of God, or to say that He may not, if He will, use the very unconscious words of wicked men as well as the heart service of pious men.

19. But farther, is it not true that Almighty God has made even acts and histories to prophesy, independently of any utterance of men's mouths ? Are there not types in the Law, and through all the Old Testament history, which have their antitypes in the New Testament ? There are those, no doubt, who will say that we can find historical parallels in profane, as readily as in sacred, history. But are these really to be compared with the sacrifice of Isaac typifying the death and resurrection of Christ—with the history of Joseph, sold by his brethren, and then exalted to be their prince and saviour—with the brazen serpent, lifted up to heal all that looked on it— with the passage of the Red Sea, and other parables put forth by the history of the Exodus—with the priesthood of Aaron, the passover, the ceremonies on the day of atonment, and the many Levitical rites forepicturing Christ—with the kingly types, such as David

and Solomon—with the prophetic parallelism of Elijah and John the Baptist—and the many others, too many to enumerate now?* If there be, as the writers of the New Testament all assert, and as Christians have ever hitherto believed, a complete system of type and antitype in the Old and New Testament respectively; to what can we attribute this, but to an overruling Hand guiding the fortunes of the chosen race, and of individuals in that race, and to the continual presence of that Holy Spirit who divideth to every man severally as He will? Is not all this to be esteemed a special inspiration? And if all this is in the Old Testament, then, whatever human elements there be in it, there is surely such a Divine element

---

* Professor Jowett thinks we must give up the types appealed to in the New Testament, just as we do not press the patristic appeal to the scarlet thread of Rahab, or the 318 followers of Abraham. That is to say, we must attach no more importance to the language of the Apostles, or of our blessed Lord Himself, than to the language of any Christian writer in the earlier days of Christianity. The New Testament has appealed to types of Christ in the Old Testament. The early Christians universally acknowledged such types, but perhaps unwisely found moreover certain fanciful resemblances unknown to the Apostles and Evangelists. Because the latter were fanciful, must we conclude that the former were false?

as to make its books emphatically the "Oracles of God," to which we may look as unmistakably embodying His will and word. We may admit that the word of God so embodied in the Scriptures was designed to communicate to us great moral and spiritual truths, that there was no purpose to give any revelation of physical science or of mere general history. Yet if we have abundant evidence that Almighty God chose the prophets and the books of the Bible as channels for communicating His will to mankind, we have surely abundant evidence that they would not be permitted to err in things pertaining to God. It may not be proof that their language will not be popular, and so possibly inaccurate, in matters of science, or that their statements will be infallible in the matter of a date or in other things immaterial; but it is surely proof enough that they would never be permitted to mislead us in questions of faith; for otherwise they would bring us credentials to their faithfulness from God Himself, and with these credentials in their hands, deceive, and mislead, and delude us.

And here may we not see the fallacy of Coleridge's view, who accepts Scripture where it "finds" him, but not in its less interesting and merely historical records? If we go on this principle, where are we to stop? If we read the second book of Chronicles, perhaps we may discover very little which "finds" us; whereas, if we read Baxter's 'Saint's Everlasting Rest,' it may "find" us in nearly every page. To carry out Coleridge's principle, we ought to uncanonize, or reject the inspiration of, the book of Chronicles, and set up as canonical the book of Baxter. But, if our former arguments be correct, and the general belief of Christians in all ages be true, the whole historical record of the Old Testament is part of the great depository of God's revealed will. One part may be more important than another. But when we see that God spoke by words of man, and also by acts of man—that even actions were predictions—when we find Christ Himself and His Apostles citing the books of the Old Testament, as the "Scriptures," as the "Oracles of God," as "God-breathed" ($\Theta\varepsilon\acute{o}\pi\nu\varepsilon\upsilon\sigma\tau\alpha$)—surely we have no right to say that one part "finds me" and another does not, and to settle our own Canon accordingly. The whole collection of the books of the Old Testament comes to us with Divine credentials — prophecies in it fulfilled after they were uttered — Christ's attestation to them, that they all testified of Him—St. Paul's testimony to them that they were " given by inspiration of God "—and, having such Divine credentials, we cannot suppose that any of these books would mislead us, at least in things heavenly.

20. If all this holds of the Old Testament, it holds, *à fortiori*, of the New ; for probably no one will contend that the Apostles, with Christ's own mission, with the gift of tongues and miraculous powers, with the special promise of the Comforter and of guidance by Him into all truth, with the assurance of Christ's own presence, and with the command to preach on the house-tops what He had told them in the ear,—were in a worse position or more liable to error than the prophets of the Old Testament. And, though we may well believe that each individual Apostle, like every Christian man, may have grown in grace and in the knowledge of our Lord and Saviour Jesus Christ ; yet this belief need in nowise interfere with our acknowledgment that messengers, specially accredited by God to man, would never be permitted to deliver a false

message, or to mislead those whom they were so signally commissioned to lead.*

For Mr. Maurice's question, as to whether

---

* Revelation has all along been progressive, but not on that account self-contradictory. Abel offered the firstlings of his flock ; Abraham offered a ram instead of his son ; Moses instituted the Paschal sacrifice ; John the Baptist pointed to " the Lamb of God, which taketh away the sin of the world ;" St. Paul spoke of " Christ our Passover ;" St. Peter of " the precious blood of Christ, as of a lamb without blemish and without spot." There is the same testimony here through a course of at least four thousand years ; but yet the knowledge was progressive. John the Baptist knew more of Christ than all that before him had been born of woman, but less than the least in the kingdom of the Saviour. What is true of the knowledge of the Church may be equally true of the knowledge of the Apostles. If they had not been capable of growth in wisdom, they would not have been human ; but no proof whatever has yet been given that the testimony of one Apostle is, on points of Christian doctrine, in conflict with the testimony of another, or that the more matured knowledge of any particular Apostle ever led him to contradict, in the least degree, his own former witness to the truth. Certainly they themselves always appeal to the consistency of their own teaching, and denounce all teaching which is inconsistent with their own. " Though we or an angel from heaven preach any other Gospel unto you than that which we have preached unto you, let him be accursed." (Gal. i. 8.) " If there come any unto you, and bring not this doctrine, receive him not into your house, neither bid him God speed." (2 John 10.)

we ought not to consider the inspiration of Holy Scripture like to that inspiration for which all of us pray, there seems but little difficulty in the reply. Undoubtedly, the inspiration for which we pray is the same as the inspiration of the writers of Scripture—that is to say, it is the inspiration of God's Holy Spirit which guides not only into holiness, but also into truth. Probably pious men in general never begin any work of importance without praying for grace and guidance; but when they do so, they do not expect to be answered with, for instance, the gift of tongues. They ask for the word of wisdom or the word of knowledge, not for the working of miracles; yet they look for it from one and the self-same Spirit. And surely we may admit that that great Teacher of the Church may teach one in one way and another in another. It may be His will to give one a deep insight into spiritual mysteries, but yet not to give him a knowledge of future events. To another, at a particular period of the Church, or under a peculiar dispensation, he may give the power of prophecy, or the gift of tongues, or the working of miracles, or such guidance and direction as shall render his testimony, as to things heavenly, infallibly true. Are we to deny that God can do so? Or again—is it impossible for him to give such a knowledge except in the way of giving a higher degree of sanctification, purifying the soul from all that may darken the understanding, and so sharpening the spiritual insight? Such a view of things is surely in direct opposition to the constant record of the Bible. If it be true, it must convict the writers of the books of the Bible of false testimony. Is it not clearly set down that Balaam—that "the man of God, who was disobedient to the word of the Lord"—that Jonah, who fled from God's presence—that Caiaphas, even when compassing Christ's crucifixion—were all empowered to speak of future things, and some of them sorely against their wills? Although it is most likely that God would in general use sanctified instruments to speak to man of sacred things, yet, if the record of the Bible be true, there may be a revelation to the mind, and so through the mouths of men, which is not the result of high sanctification, of purifying the heart that it may see God. A man may have "the gift of prophecy and understand all mysteries and all knowledge," may "speak with the tongues of men and angels," and yet lack charity and be nothing.

21. And so, to pass to another view of the question, Mr. Morell argues that the Divine or religious truth can only be revealed to our highest and deepest intuitional consciousness. It is not to be received by the senses, by the understanding, or by the reason, but deeper down still in our inmost being. There is no reason to quarrel with this statement so far as it goes. Its fault is, that it is one-sided. "When it pleased God to reveal his Son in" St. Paul, doubtless the revelation was not to the intellect only, but to the very heart of hearts. But there may be abundant head-knowledge without any such revelation to the soul and spirit. And must we not distinguish here between objective and subjective revelation? Of course objective revelation must suppose a subject; that is to say, if an object is to be revealed, there must be a subject by which that object may be embraced and conceived. But is it not plain to common-sense, setting aside all logical subtilty, that there may be an uotward manifesting ($\varphi\alpha\nu\acute{\epsilon}\rho\omega\sigma\iota\varsigma$, if $\grave{\alpha}\pi o\kappa\acute{\alpha}\lambda\upsilon\psi\iota\varsigma$ be ambiguous) of God to man, without any inward reception of Him to the soul? And if so, may not a man be taught, as Daniel or St. John, by a vision of God, and yet, like Balaam or Jonah, not have his soul con

verted to God? He may "see the vision of the Almighty, falling into a trance, and having his eyes open;" and yet his heart may not be opened to know and to love God. It really seems as if Mr. Maurice, Mr. Morell, and others of similar sentiments, deny the possibility of this.* But on what principle can it be denied, except on a principle which rejects all that is miraculous, and which makes God, not a Personal Being, but an impersonal influence?

22. But if we believe that God has in different ages authorized certain persons to communicate objective truth to mankind, if in the Old Testament history and the books of the prophets we find manifest indications of the Creator, it is then a secondary consideration, and a question on which we may safely agree to differ, whether or not every book of the Old Testament was written so completely under the dictation of God's Holy Spirit, that every word, not only doctrinal, but also historical or scientific, must be infallibly correct

* Of course, Professor Baden Powell must have held this impossible, because he held that there was no contact point between the spiritual and the physical worlds. They lie, according to him, in two distinct planes, which can never come in contact. But to what must such a theory lead short of Materialism and Atheism, in minds of the common stamp?

and true. The whole collection of the books has been preserved providentially to the Church as the record of God's early dealings with mankind, and especially with one chosen race, as the collection of the prophecies and of the religious instruction which God was pleased to communicate to man in the preparatory dispensations of His grace : and with these there is a book of sacred psalmody, embodying the religious experience of men living under the Theocracy, some at least of the hymns contained in it evincing the power of prophecy in their writers. Whatever conclusion, then, may be arrived at as to the infallibility of the writers on matters of science or of history, still the whole collection of the books will be really the oracles of God, the Scriptures of God, the record and depository of God's supernatural revelations in early times to man. And we may remember that our Blessed Lord quotes the Psalms as the Scripture, adding, "And the Scripture cannot be broken."

23. It has been already observed that what holds good of the Old Testament holds *à fortiori* of the New. If the writers of it were the accredited messengers from God to man, taught by Christ, assured by Him of the teach-

ing of His Holy Spirit, sent to bring to man the knowledge of God and of His highest truths, we cannot doubt that that Spirit, who was to guide them into all truth, would never let them err in things pertaining to God. This is really what we want. We want to be assured that we have an *infallible* depository of *religious* truth. And if we are satisfied that the Apostles were accredited messengers for delivering God's message and communicating God's truth to the world, clearly we have this assurance. It may, no doubt, be true that all ministers of Christ in all ages are God's accredited messengers; but the difference is this: the Apostles had new truths to deliver direct from heaven; other ministers of Christ have old truths to impress—truths which may perhaps be new to their hearers, but which are old to the Church. In the one case there is a direct commission with a need of infallibility in things spiritual; in the other the mission is through the intervention of others, and with the power of correcting errors by appealing to the authority of the written record.

If we can establish this much then, there seems no need to fear the admission of a human element, as well as a Divine, in Scripture. The Apostles had the treasure of the

Gospel in earthen vessels. The Holy Spirit taught the Churches through the instrumentality of men of like passions with ourselves. The difficulty of enunciating a definite theory of inspiration consists exactly in this—in assigning the due weight respectively to the Divine and the human elements. A human element there clearly was. Though in instances like those of Balaam and Caiaphas we seem to have something more like organic inspiration, yet in ordinary cases God was pleased to take the nobler instruments of man's thoughts and hearts through which to communicate a knowledge of Himself to the world, rather than to act through the organs of speech moving men's mouths as mere machines. With all the pains and ingenuity which have been bestowed upon the subject, no charge of error, even in matters of human knowledge, has ever yet been substantiated against any of the writers of Scripture. But, even if it had been otherwise, is it not conceivable that there might have been infallible Divine teaching in all things spiritual and heavenly, whilst on mere matters of history, or of daily life, Prophets and Evangelists might have been suffered to write as men? Even if this were true, we need not be perplexed or disquieted, so we can be agreed that the Divine element was ever such as to secure the infallible truth of Scripture in all things Divine.

24. All this, of course, is applicable to questions of physical science. Scripture was not given to teach us science, but to teach us religion; it may not have been needful that the inspired writers should have been rendered infallible in matters of science, nor is it at all likely that they should have been directed to teach to the ancient world truths which would anticipate the discoveries either of Newton or of Cuvier. It would have been almost as strange if they had not used popular expressions in writing on such subjects, as if they had written not in the tongue of their own people, but in a new dialect more refined and philosophical. But may we not ask, whether in this question of physical science, as in many like things, sceptical writers have not been sharp-sighted on minute discrepancies, whilst they have been blind to the great general harmony of truth? It is ever so; each petty difference of date, each little inconsistency in two concurrent narratives, every, the slightest appearance of doubtful morality, anything like a supposed repugnance to what we consider the necessary attributes of the Most

High, have been dwelt on and magnified, and used as objections to the inspiration of Holy Writ ; whilst the general truth of its history, the purity and holiness of its general moral teaching, the grandeur and sublimity of its doctrines concerning God, are altogether forgotten or concealed. Yet is it not true that, both in moral and in physical science, nothing short of miraculous inspiration can account for the superior knowledge of the writers of the Old Testament compared with the most enlightened sages of heathen antiquity ? The Jewish philosophers, like Philo, felt that the Scriptures of their own prophets had brought in simple language to their unlettered fellow-countrymen moral and spiritual truths, after which the Platonists had been "seeking, if haply they might feel after them and find them." Greeks, like Justin Martyr, who had tried one school of philosophy after another, discovered in the Gospel all that was most valuable in the teaching of all schools. And may not we, who have come upon an age of rapid discovery in physical science, confess that the account given of the Creator and His works in the Bible was an anticipation and is an epitome of all that has lately come to light ? The telescope has revealed to us worlds and systems of worlds rolling in unbroken order through infinity of space; the microscope has shown us living and organized beings so small as to bewilder the mind with their minuteness as the suns and planets bewilder it with their vastness; the geologist takes us back through countless ages, the records of which are indelibly engraven " as with lead in the rock for ever." And the Bible, but no other ancient book that is written, had told us that the Being who created all things was such that the Heaven and the Heaven of Heavens could not contain Him, that He was the High and lofty One inhabiting eternity, but that though He had His dwelling so high, yet He humbled Himself to behold the things that are in heaven and earth, that a sparrow did not fall without Him, that the very hairs of man's head were numbered by Him. Infinite greatness, infinite minuteness, infinity of duration, infinity of action, eternity of past existence and of past operation, as well as an eternity of the future, are all distinctly predicated in the Scriptures of the mind of Him who made us all. And here for the first time, now in the nineteenth century, we find the same infinity in heaven and in earth, and in the sea, and under the earth.

Why, then, must we be puzzled because some recently discovered geological phenomena seem hard to reconcile with a few verses in one chapter of Genesis? Are we to forget the marvellous harmony between God's word and His works, which a general view of both convinces us of, because there are some small fragments of both, which we have not yet learned to fit into each other? Nay! even here, we may fairly say, that the harmony already found is greater than the as yet unexplained discord. For, putting aside all doubtful interpretations and difficult questions concerning the six days of creation and the like, these two facts are certain; all sound criticism and all geological inquiry prove them alike; viz., first, that the original creation of the universe was at a period indefinitely, if not infinitely, distant from the present time; and secondly, that of all animated beings, the last that came into existence was man. Geology has taught us both these facts; but the first verse of Genesis clearly teaches the first, and the twenty-sixth verse teaches the second.

To touch but for a moment on one other subject which has been so strongly pressed of late, the uniform prevalence of law, not only in things inanimate, but where there is life and even reason and morality—can anything be more consistent than this with the whole of the Old Testament ? Indeed its peculiar teaching from first to last may be said to have been that God is a God of order ; that He has impressed His law on all creation ; that all things serve Him, all things obey Him ; that to break laws, whether moral or physical, is inevitably to entail suffering ; and that even rational and spiritual beings, even in their rational and spiritual natures and capacities, are subject to laws which cannot be broken ; that the sins of the fathers go down in sin and sorrow to the children ; and that even repentance, though it may save the soul, cannot undo the sin or avert the suffering. There is nowhere in creation or in history written more plainly the record of order and law.

25. Surely such thoughts as these seem fit to satisfy us, that God's works rightly read are not likely to contradict God's word rightly interpreted. There will be for a time, perhaps for all time, apparent difficulties. When new questions arise, at first many will feel that it is hopeless to attempt to solve them. Some will despair, some will try to smother inquiry ; some will rush into Atheism, and others will fall back into superstition. Patience is the

proper temper for an age like our own, which is in many ways an age of transition. The discoveries of Galileo seemed more alarming to his contemporaries than any discoveries in geology or statistics can seem to us. We see no difficulty in Galileo's discoveries now. Such things, then, are probably the proper trials of our faith. Sober views, patience, prayer, a life of godliness, and a good conscience, will, no doubt, keep us from making shipwreck of faith. What now seems like a shadow may only be the proof that there is a light behind it. And even if at times there should come shadows seeming like deep night, we may hope that the dawn of the morning is but the nearer.

SCRIPTURE, AND ITS INTERPRETATION.

CONTENTS.

SECT. 1. THE ALLEGED VARIATIONS IN THE INTERPRETATION OF SCRIPTURE, p. 425.
1. Introductory comments and definitions.
2. Present attitude and expectations.
3. Amount of varying interpretations much exaggerated—as shown by *first*, Ancient and modern versions; *secondly*, Comparison of earlier and later expositions.
4. Literal and historical mode of interpretation adopted from the first.
5. Recapitulation.

SECT. 2. THE CHARACTERISTICS OF SCRIPTURE, p. 445.
6. Differences of interpretation in details.
7. This diversity in unity to be accounted for—I. By the difference of the Bible from every other Book. II. By the fact that Scripture often involves more than one meaning: as shown by (1) Applications of prophecy, (2) Types, (3) Deeper meanings, even in historical passages. III. By the fact that Scripture is divinely inspired.
8. Examination of the assertions of opponents concerning the Inspiration of Scripture, as regards, *first*, the Testimony of Scripture in reference to itself; *secondly*, the Statements of the Early Church; *thirdly*, the Subjective testimony.
9. Affirmative observations upon Inspiration—Considerations concerning, *first*, its Mode; *secondly*, its Limits; *thirdly*, its Degree.
10. Recapitulation.

SECT. 3. GENERAL RULES OF INTERPRETATION, p. 480.
11. Preliminary comments—Duty of Prayer—Necessity for candor.
12. Rules for the Interpretation of Scripture—First Rule—*Interpret grammatically*—Examples. Second Rule—*Interpret historically*—Examples. Third Rule—*Interpret Contextually*—Examples. Fourth Rule—*Interpret minutely*—Examples. Failure of these rules in cases of difficulty. Gradual emergence of supplementary rules. Fifth Rule - *Interpret according to the analogy of faith.*
13. Concluding observations.

SECT. 4. THE APPLICATION OF SCRIPTURE, p. 513.
14. Application of Scripture considered in reference to, I. Prophecy and Typology. II. Second and deeper meanings. III. Practical and special deductions.

SECT. 5. GRAMMAR AND THE LAWS OF THE LETTER, p. 522.
15. Introductory remarks.
16. General character of the language of the New Testament, as compared with earlier and later Greek.
17. Peculiarities as shown in details, especially in reference to (1) the Article, (2) Substantives, (3) Verbs, (4) Prepositions, (5) Particles.
18. Conclusion.

SCRIPTURE, AND ITS INTERPRETATION.

I.

1. It can hardly be considered strange that great differences of opinions hould exist respecting the interpretation of Scripture. When we consider the nature of the Sacred Writings, their number, their variety, the different epochs to which they belong, and the vast period of time over which they extend, we can hardly be surprised to find the opinions concerning the interpretation of the Volume into which they are collected not only to be various, but even conflicting. When we turn from the outward to the inward, and ponder over "that inexhaustible and infinite character" of the Sacred Writings, which even the better portion of our opponents are not unwilling to concede,—when we observe that "depth and inwardness," which, it has been rightly con-

sidered, require something corresponding in the interpreter himself,—when we reverentially recognize throughout the Volume references alike to the past, the present, and the future ; teachings in history only partly realized, lessons in prophecy " not yet learned even in theory," germs of truth which, we are told, have yet to take root in the world,—when we consider all this, are we to wonder that differences of opinion exist concerning the interpretation of a volume so ancient, so wondrous, and so multiform ?

It would indeed be strange if it had been otherwise ; it would be a phenomenon in the literary or mental history of Christianity not easy to account for, if expounders of Scripture had been found always accordant in their views ; nay, it may even be considered a subject for surprise, though for thankfulness, that the differences of opinion about the interpretation of a volume such as we have described are not greater than we find them to be.

When, however, we are thus speaking of the differences of opinion respecting the interpretation of Scripture (and we are using the language of opponents), let us, from the very outset, agree to avoid all ambiguities in language. Let us be careful not to fall into an error which we may fairly impute to those with whom we are contending,—the error, to choose the mildest expression, of using terms of a vague and undefined character, and, as the sequel will show, of a somewhat convenient elasticity. What do we mean by differences respecting the interpretation of Scripture? We may mean two things. Either we may mean that there have been differences of opinion about the meanings of the actual words of Scripture, or we may mean that there have been differences of opinion about the manner in which those meanings have been obtained. We may include both if we choose in the same forms of words, but in so doing let us not fail to apprise the reader, and in conducting the argument let us act with fairness. Let us be careful to recognize the clear logical difference between these two meanings, and avoid that really culpable method of dealing with a momentous subject which does not scruple to mix up illustrations or arguments derived from one of its aspects with those which really and plainly belong to the other. There may have been from the very first many methods of interpreting Scripture: allegory may have prevailed in one age, mysticism in another; scholastic methods of interpretation may have been succeeded by rhetorical, and these again may both have given place to methods in which grammar and history may have borne a more prominent part. All this may have been so, but it still does not necessarily follow that the meanings actually assigned to any given text have been as manifold or as discordant as the methods which may have been adopted to obtain them. The modes and principles of interpretation may have been very different, and yet, in the main, they may have led to very accordant results. Such a probability, however, is now somewhat studiously passed over in silence, or mentioned only to be dismissed as unworthy of serious consideration. The object, we fear, is to create anxiety and uneasiness, to unfix and to unloosen, to awaken a general feeling of distrust in current interpretations, and, in the case of doctrinal statements and every form of exposition that involves a reference to the analogy of faith, to arouse even hostility and antagonism. This has been done of late, as we have already implied, by a judicious combination of two methods of proceeding,—on the one hand, by calling attention to the discordances of interpretation in a few extreme cases where such discordance is sure to be a maximum; on the other, by dwelling exclusively on the varieties of the different systems and methods of interpretation, and leaving it to be inferred that the results arrived at are as various and diversified as the methods by which they have been obtained. In a word, such a phenomenon as a Catholic interpretation, substantially the same under all systems, but varied only in details or application, is assumed to be an exegetical impossibility. The true state of the case we are told is this,—that Scripture has had every possible variety of meaning assigned to it, that it has been understood to say this to one age and that to another, that all hitherto has been conflict or uncertainty. We learn, however, that now a better era is dawning; that a fundamental principle, viz., that Scripture has one meaning and one meaning only, has at length clearly been made out; and that a little "free handling," a few assumptions, and a free use of a so-called "verifying faculty," will finally adjust all difficulties and discordances in the interpretation of the Book of Life.

There is obviously something very attractive in all this. There is a fascination in the whole procedure that imperfectly disciplined or willingly sceptical minds find it impossible to resist. There is the charm of the alleged discovery that criticism at last has made, the attractiveness of the generalization, the variety of the modes of applying the principle so as to meet all needs, whether of the reader, the preacher, the missionary, the teacher, or the interpreter,—and then the retrospect, the backward look of serene triumph over the accumulated errors and prejudices of eighteen long Christian centuries, all chased away by the brightness of this second Reformation and the " burst of intellectual life" that is at last becoming visible above the clouded horizon of Scriptural interpretation. One topmost stone, and the monument of our exegetical successes must be pronounced complete. Philosophy and Theology claim of us, we are told, as of value to themselves a history of the past. Be it so. Let us take the pen of the historian and sit down and trace the record of our own mental supremacy in a history of the prejudices and errors of the Exegesis of the past. Let us show by this tacit comparison how " great names must be accounted small," how few ever " bent their mind to interrogate the meaning of words," how men who were accounted benefactors of the human race have yet only left to us the heritage of erring fancies and party-bias,—let us write the history of all this littleness, confusion, and bondage to the letter, and the fabric of our own greatness, harmony, and intellectual freedom will appear by the contrast only the more stately and unique.

Such is the dream of the present. Such, stated in no exaggerated or unkindly terms, is the course which men whose general goodness and high principles we have no cause to doubt or deny are now inviting us to follow. What are we to say of all this? The comment rises to the lips, but we suppress it. We may feel, perhaps, that as in Corinth of old so now in nineteenth-century England, vain knowledge may puff up, yet remembering that "love edifieth," we sit by silent and wondering, even though the fire is kindling within, and silence is becoming a pain and a grief to us. At first perhaps we prepare to answer the call to join the wise and tranquil few, who, knowing that the Eternal Spirit has been ever present with the Church, and that what things were written aforetime were written, not for our contempt but for our learning, smile pensively at these childish exultations and straw-woven crowns, and see in them only one more of the premature triumphs that have been claimed for some shifting form of the errors or heresies of the time. We feel tempted to join this quiet company, and calmly to smile as they alone can smile whose feet stand within the sheltering walls of the City of God, and whose faith is that which was not only delivered but handed down to the saints in each age of the Church of Christ. What can we do but smile, when we recognize old quibbles and difficulties all mustered up again, disguised in new trappings, and arranged in new combinations, —but yet the same, the very same that have been dispersed a hundred times over, and which the very generation to which we now belong will see dispersed again, though it may be to ally themselves finally with powers and principles of which at present they are only permitted to act as the scout and the courier?

But with this last thought the smile fades away. When we remember that the forms of error which of late have been reappearing among us may belong, consciously or unconsciously, to the great apostasy of the future,—when we observe how they instinctively associate themselves with masked or avowed denyings of the Divinity of our blessed Lord, and of the full efficacy of His sacrifice,—when we mark how their vanities and self-confidences bear a strange family likeness to that Pelagian pride in the perfectibility of our corrupted nature which tears open the wounds of a crucified Lord more heartlessly than the hands that first inflicted them,—when we ponder over that puffed up and unyoked spirit of the day that is now calling on us to clear away the remains of dogmas and controversies, and when we see, as we must see, with a shudder, that it is but the harbinger of him who is to set himself against everything "that is called God or that is worshipped" (2 Thess. ii. 4),—then it does seem our duty to play our part in the great controversy, to quit ourselves like men, and to strive with all Christian earnestness, with stern brow yet with true and loving heart, to secure the endangered souls of our own time and age, and to bring them back into the City of God.

2. The position of the defender of the faith in the present day is that of one whose home and citizenship is in the City "that lieth four-square," whose builder and whose maker is God. The storm of battle has often raged round those massive walls, wild rout and turmoil have often striven to shake those solid gates. Passwords have been tried; treachery has played its dastardly part,—but all stands firm and sure. The rising sun that smites on

the broad front of those fair walls and towers, beholds them as stately in their strength and their beauty as they were ever of old; the shadows they cast when day declines are as many and as lengthened as they were of yore. Who within would wish to see a stone displaced, who would fain see one battlement laid low? Perhaps none who are really and truly within the circuit of those sheltering walls. But there are voices without that we know full well, voices of those with whom we have dwelt as friends, whose God has been our God, and whose Lord has been our Lord,—men who went from among us on strange missions, and are come back to tell us strange tidings, and to bid us do strange deeds. That beleaguering host whose flaunting standards we can see on every wooded knoll around, and whose open or covert assaults our fathers and forefathers have experienced so often, and resisted so successfully and so long,—that motley eager host they tell us is not composed of foes but of friends and well-wishers, changed by civilization and the glory of human development, eager to meet us as kindred and brothers if we will but remove the envious barriers that separate us, relics of a religious feudalism, as they term it, long passed away. Shall creeds separate brothers? Shall doctrines divide those whom unity of race and shared civilizations plainly declare to be one and inseparable? Shall we churlishly strive any longer to stint the growth of the ideal man? Shall the orient and glowing future be darkened with jealousies of sects and rivalries of religions? "We are couriers," they impetuously cry aloud; "ambassadors, friends of both, friends of truth, friends of Christ. Unbar, then, these envious gates; down with these unfriendly walls; let us learn from each other the great lesson of mutual concessions, and so at last realize the great hope of the future, the fabled restitution of theologians, and at last, all in fraternal triumph, merge into the one great family of Truth and of Love." Such are the voices now sounding in our ears; voices that the young and the generous, as well as the godless and the worldworn, give ear to with ready sympathy. But shall the true defenders of the ark of their God, that ark of the New Covenant wherein lie the written words of life, yield it and themselves up to this stratagem which one " whose time is short " has put into the hearts of unconscious instruments? Never: God defend us from such fearful, such frantic disloyalty! God indeed forbid that, in any sense, however modified, it should hereafter be the boast of the spirits of perdition, that it was with the City of the hills even worse than it was with a city of the plain,—that the host wound round it, that sounding brass brayed forth and eager voices shouted, and that, mined by traitorous occupants, wall and tower fell flat as those of Jericho, and fell never to rise again!

Such, it would seem, is the allegory of our own times—such no overdrawn picture of the exact attitude in which true believers now appear to stand. We are called upon by specious words to give up every defence which the mercies of God have permitted to be reared up around us; and our reward is to be a bondage, to which the bondage of the worst age of the Church of Rome would be found light and endurable. There is no bondage like that of scepticism. There is no intolerance more intolerable than that of those who are themselves the servants of a hard master. It may be a bondage different to bondages of the past in its mode of being brought about, but it is no less complete and coercive. It is the bondage of contempt and of scorn. Do we doubt it? Are there not writings of our own times, writings that claim scholars and ministers of the Gospel for their authors, that show, only too painfully, what we have to expect if we allow such to be leaders of thought among us, if wall and tower are to be thrown down to let such men come in and have the rule over us? Granted that there may be numerous exceptions, that there may be those who, even while we are compelled to number them among our secret foes, we may be free to own have many kindly and elevated sympathies,—granted that there may be silver sounds heard amid all this clanging brass, yet does not common sense, does not history itself tell us, that the voices of this better part will be the first to be silenced; that their kindly idealisms will be rudely swept aside to make room for varied and repulsive forms of aggressive materialism; that they will themselves be the earliest victims of the Frankenstein their own hands have helped to shape into existence? Let the thoughtful reader pause only for a moment to muse upon some of the present aspects of modern society as revealed by, as commented on, and sometimes even as defended by, our public papers, and then answer to his own heart what he thinks must be the issue if laxity of religious thought seriously increase among us. Vice will borrow its excuses from scepticism; lawlessness of act will become the natural sequel of lawlessness of thought; and the end will be, no noble, colossal, heavenward-looking, ideal man, but a grovelling satyr, the slave of his own appetites, and the vassal of his own abominations.

But we must pass on to, or rather return to, the subject which lies more immediately before us. Enough, perhaps, has been said to show that there can be no safe compromise, no over-liberal parleying with those without, be they the kindliest or the most silver-tongued of the children of men. The believer of the present day must put himself in the attitude of an opponent, kind indeed it may be, and large in heart and sympathies, ready and anxious to rescue, prompt to spare,—yet an opponent; one who, when asked to give up old principles, may not, for the sake of others, wholly refuse to hear the nature of the demand, but who hears it with a full knowledge of the true attitude and posture of those by whom it is urged. We are asked especially to give up old principles in the interpretation of the Word of God. Some concession, we are warned, is almost imperatively demanded. We ask why. We bid our opponents state their reasons for a demand so sweeping and comprehensive. One of these reasons we have heard already, and we have already observed that it involves an ambiguity. We are told that the differences respecting the interpretation of Scripture are such that they show that prejudice rather than principle is the true mainspring of Scriptural exegesis. Pictures are held up to us of the successive schools of interpreters, their follies and their fallacies, their bondage to the influences of the age in which they lived, their hostility to all intellectual freedom. Be it so; but is it proved that the interpretations which they actually advanced are as varied as their methods of procedure are so confidently alleged to be? Whether a great deal too much has not been said even on this subject, whether the diversities or antagonisms of early systems of explaining Scripture have not been greatly exaggerated, is a question into which here we will not enter. Our inquiry is simply, whether the differences of interpretation are at all more than the nature and importance of the subject-matter would lead us to expect, and whether a great deal that has been said about the differences of interpretation does not wholly belong to the differences of the modes of procedure. It is, of course, quite natural and conceivable that the spirit of each age may have swayed teacher and preacher more to this method than to that; that passing controversies may have left their traces, and that declarations which seemed of great moment to one generation may not have been found equally so to another. All this may be so, but with this we are now only partially concerned. If we were endeavoring to form an estimate of the variety of deductions that have been made from the words of Scripture in different ages of the Church, or were discussing the varying applications that the same sentiment has been found to bear, much that has been said on the subject might pass unchallenged. We should probably account for these varied forms of application or deduction on different principles to our opponents; we might see, for instance, in all this diversity of application only evidences of "the manifold wisdom of God," and of that hidden life with all its varying aptitudes to human needs which we know to be in the Written Word. Our opponents, on the contrary, might see in it only evidences of the folly, ignorance, prejudice, or bad faith of successive expositors: we might differ widely in our manner of accounting for these different applications of Scripture, but we might to a great extent agree as to their number and variety. This, however, is not the question between us. What we are now told is not merely that the applications or adaptations of Scripture have been very varied, but that the difference of actual meaning assigned to the words of Scripture by expositors of different ages is so suspiciously excessive, that the duty of purging our minds from past prejudices is imperative, and that Scripture must henceforth be explained on sounder principles. The one true meaning must be discovered and adopted, the many disregarded or rejected. The first question between us, then, is a question of amount and of degree. Our opponents assert that Scripture has had so many meanings, often too so hostile and suicidal, that it presents one meaning to the Frenchman, another to the German, and another to the Englishman. We are asked if this is not in itself an utter absurdity, and if it is not time to enter upon some more reasonable course. That assumed reasonable course is sketched out; canons of interpretation are laid down; appeals are not wanting to current prejudices; disinclination or inaptitude for that wrestling with the Word of God which marked earlier and better ages of the Church is dealt gently with; disregard of the great exegetical writings of the past is not only excused but commended; we are advised wholly to trust to ourselves, and are cheered by the assurance that " if we will only confine ourselves to the plain meaning of words and the study of their context," we may beneficially dispense with all the expository labors of the past or of the present. Such is the modern mode of dealing with one of the most momentous subjects of our own times, and with which personal holiness and man's salvation are more intimately connected than with any other that can be specified. Is it unfair to characterize the whole as nothing more than positive assertions, resting on ambiguities of language, or on the assumed identity of things logically different, and supported by covert appeals to the idleness, vanity, and self-sufficiency of the day?

3. We revert, however, to the preliminary question before us. Are the differences of meaning that have been assigned to Scripture such in amount as they are said to be, and such as to demand the rehabilitation of Scriptural interpretation which is now proposed? Are they such that, as it has been asserted, Scripture bears an utterly different meaning to men of different ages and nations? Assuredly not. No statement seems more completely at

variance with our general Christian consciousness; no assertion can more readily be disapproved when we come to details. These, however, can never be made palatable to the general reader, nor are they commonly convincing, unless carried out much further than would be possible in an Essay of this nature. To prove clearly and distinctly that there is *not* this great amount of discordance in the interpretations of Scripture, it would be necessary to compare, and that not in a few selected cases, but in a portion of Scripture of some length, the results arrived at by commentators of different ages and countries. Less than this would fail to convince; for in the case of a few prerogative instances, which would be all we should have space for, the feeling is ever apt to arise that lists equally telling and convincing could be made out on the other side We have, therefore, as it would seem, little left us than to meet assertion by counter-assertion, and leave each reader to ascertain for himself on which side the truth lies,—whether the differences in the interpretations of Scripture (except in a comparatively few cases) have been thus excessive, or whether there has not been a very considerable amount of accordance in general matters, and variations only in de tails. Those who are acquainted with the subject, and have had experience in referring to expository treatises belonging to different ages and countries, will have no difficulty in pronouncing which is the true state of the case, and whether assertion or counter-assertion is to be deemed most worthy of credit. As, however, the general reader is not always likely to have it in his power to decide between the two statements, and as the mere denial of the major in an opponent's syllogism is never satisfactory without some reasons being assigned, we will mention one or two general considerations which, though not amounting to a positive proof that Scripture has *not* been interpreted as diversely as has been asserted, may yet render it probable that such is the case, and supply some grounds for the counter-assertion above alluded to.

In the first place, we may perhaps with justice appeal to the Ancient Versions, especially when combined with some of the best Modern Versions, as tending to show that the amount of variety in interpretation is not so great as has been imagined. Let us take, for example, seven of the best Ancient Versions of the New Testament—the Syriac (Peshito), the Old Latin (as far as it has been ascertained), the Vulgate, the Gothic, the Coptic, the Ethiopic (Pell Platt's), and the Armenian, and with them let us associate the Authorized English Version and Luther's German Version, and then proceed to inquire what general opinion a comparison of the characteristics of these Versions leads us to form as to the question of a prevailing unanimity, or a prevailing discordance, of interpretation, as far as it can be evinced by a Version. Now, admitting on the one hand that there may be such relations existing between some of these Versions, that each can hardly be considered an independent witness,—that the Vulgate, for example, is but an amended form of the Old Latin, that the Ethiopic sometimes seems to indicate dependence on the Syriac, that the Armenian was retouched at a late period, and possibly that the Vulgate was in the hands of the reviser,—admitting all this, and making also a deduction for the influence of the Vulgate, and, perhaps, to some small extent, of the Syriac over the two modern Versions, we may still most justly point to these nine Versions, of ages and countries so different and distant, as evincing an unanimity in their renderings, not only of general but even of disputed passages, far beyond what could have been expected *à priori*, or can in any way be accounted for by the admissions we have already made. If it be said this must necessarily be the case in Versions which are all strictly literal in their character, these two remarks may be made by way of rejoinder: first, that the very fact that nine Versions of different ages and countries should agree in this important feature, that not one of them should in any respect be paraphrastic,* and that some, as for instance the Old Latin, should almost be barbarous in their exactness, does seem to show that not only in later ages, but even in the earliest, the very letter of Scripture was regarded as of the utmost importance, and treated with the most scrupulous accuracy. Where versions were so punctilious, it does not seem natural to expect that interpretation would have been very wild or varied, except when it was allowed to degenerate into applications, or busied itself with minutiæ and details. Secondly, it may be added, that even the most literal Versions involve interpreta-

---

* It may be noticed that we have specified the Ethiopic Version as that edited by Mr. Pell Platt. The Ethiopic found in Walton's 'Polyglot' often degenerates into a paraphrase, especially in difficult passages. The Peshito is sometimes idiomatically free, but never paraphrastic.

tion in the fullest sense of the word, especially in the opinions they necessarily express on the connexion of clauses, and in the renderings of words of disputed meaning. A good translation is often the very best of commentaries, and it was a full appreciation of this fact that led a venerated scholar and divine, when asked what he judged to be the best commentary on the New Testament, to name the Vulgate. The general unanimity of the early as well as later Versions is thus a testimony, at any rate, of some little weight, in favor of the belief that the amount and degree of differences of interpretation in earlier, when compared with later ages, have been much overstated.

Still it may be urged, that whatever may be the case with Versions, it is perfectly certain that, in the results at which commentators of different ages have arrived, there is a vast amount not only of variety but of antagonism. In reference to a certain number of difficult passages this may be true; if, however, this be intended as a general statement referring to Scriptural interpretation at large, it must be regarded as open to considerable doubt. Let us endeavor to show this in the following way. It is said that there is an increasing agreement between recent German expositors, and it is also implied that the results at which they have arrived are far more consonant with truth than any that have preceded. Of these expositors, De Wette and Meyer are often mentioned with respect by modern writers. Let us agree to take them as two fair representatives of the exegesis of our own times. Let us now go to a remote past, and choose two names to compare with them as representatives of the interpretation of a former day. Let us take for example Chrysostom and Theodoret. They belonged to an age sufficiently distant; they shared in its feelings and sympathies; they took part in its controversies. They were not specially in advance of their own times. One of them had, what many will judge to be not always compatible with calmness of interpretation, a strongly rhetorical bias; the other did not escape some suspicion of heresy. Such as they were, or have been judged to be, let us compare them, in some portion of Scripture (St. Paul's Epistles for example), on which all have written, with the two modern commentators above specified, and state what seem to be the general results of the comparison. We naturally set out with the expectation of finding very great diversity. If all that has been said on this subject be true; if the fourteen centuries which lie between the two pairs of men be as plentifully diversified as they are said to have been by changes in methods of interpretation,— changes, too, asserted to have been gradually leading us up to more perfect principles of interpretation,—we must expect to find a very great amount of discordance between them. Yet what do we discover when we actually institute the comparison? To speak very generally, it would seem to be as follows. There will be found in the first place a considerable amount of variety in matters of detail, the older interpreters more commonly giving what may be termed an objective reference to words and expressions, where the two modern writers will be found agreeing to adopt a more subjective view. In the second place, differences will be observed in the treatment of doctrinal passages; the older interpreters usually expounding them with reference to the great controversies of their own times, and to points of polemical detail; the modern interpreters usually trying to generalize, and not unfrequently to dilute and explain away, whenever doctrinal statements appear to assume a very distinctive or definite aspect. In a word, the tendency of the two earlier writers is to what is objective and special; of the two later to what is subjective and general. These distinctions will certainly be observed, especially in the two departments above alluded to—matters of detail and matters of doctrine, and may perhaps be deemed sufficient to justify the recognition of some clear lines of demarcation between earlier and more modern interpretation. When, however, these points of difference are set aside, there will be found remaining in the great bulk of Scripture, and in all general passages, an amount of accordance so striking and so persistent, that it can only be accounted for by the assumption that these four able expositors all instinctively recognized one common and sound principle of Scriptural interpretation. The precise nature of that principle will become apparent as we advance further in our investigations.

4. Believing that these remarks are just, and capable of being fully substantiated, we may claim to have at least made it probable, that the extent of the alleged differences in the interpretation of Scripture between our own times and the past has been unduly exaggerated. Here we might pause as far as the present portion of our subject is concerned. It may be well, however, to take one step fur-

ther, and show, what fairly can be shown, that from the very earliest times, the literal and historical method of interpreting Scripture, now so often claimed as the distinguishing characteristic of our own times, has ever been recognized in the Church as the true method on man's side of interpreting the Oracles of God. On this subject, owing to the small amount of exact knowledge, even among more professed students, and to the currency which a few popular comments readily obtain among those whose acquaintance with these ancient writers must ever be second-hand, many questionable statements are allowed to pass unchallenged. It would, perhaps, seem hopeless to attempt to say one word in favor of the method of interpretation adopted by Origen. Every writer of the day uses that great name to illustrate what is to be regarded as wild and fanciful. And yet, what is the opinion which any real student of Origen's exegetical works would certainly give us? What, for instance, would be the statement of an unbiassed scholar who had thoughtfully read what remain to us of his commentaries on St. Matthew and St. John? Would he not tell us that in these portions of his works, whatever may have been his theories elsewhere, Origen rarely failed to give the first place to the simple and literal intrepretation, and that his divergencies into allegory far more often deserve the name of applications than of actual expositions? Allegory seems really and primarily to have commended itself to Origen as the readiest method of dealing with those difficulties which his acute mind almost too quickly recognized as transcending human reason and explanation. The remark of one who has carefully read and well used one portion of his works—the expositor Lücke—is probably not wholly unjust, that a tendency to rationalize, of which Origen himself was unconscious, may to a great degree account for his bias to allegory and mystical modes of interpretation, whenever the difficulties of the passage seemed to rise above the usual level. Where there was no necessity for this, where there were no historical details which seemed at issue with human reason, or with received views of morality and justice, Origen shows plainly enough what method of interpreting the Word of God he deemed to be the true and correct one. We may abundantly verify this from his extant writings. We may also further judge from fragments preserved in Catenæ (his scattered comments, for example, on the Epistle to the

Ephesians) what were really his leading principles ; and we may fairly ask if they were so very different from the principles of interpreting Scripture which all parties, friends and foes, seem now in the main agreed in regarding as reasonable and correct.

We might extend these remarks almost indefinitely by discussing the true nature of the leading methods of interpreting Scripture—these methods which we are told are so strangely discordant—in the case of each one of the more distinguished expositors of different ages of the Church. We might show, for instance, that no amount of strong polemical bias prevented Cyril of Alexandria from expounding portions of Scripture (the Gospel of St. John for example) with what, even in our own critical days, must be called felicity and success. We might make it clear that the rhetorical turn of Chrysostom's mind never prevented him from fully discussing verbal distinctions, analyzing the meanings of prepositions, estimating the force of compound forms, and so placing before his reader as calm, clear, and persuasive a view of the passage under consideration as we may find in the best specimens of modern interpretation. We might turn to the West, and in spite of some growing disposition to admit more generally those studied distinctions in reference to threefold or fourfold senses of Scripture which Origen bequeathed to his successors, we might still appeal to Augustine as a writer, whose special interpretations can never be spoken of without respect, and whose perceptions of the inner mind of Scripture, and of the true bearing of its deeper declarations, remain to this very hour unequalled for their perspicuity and truth. Nay, we might even show that the studied recognition of several senses in Scripture was rather a form of *application* than of definite and genuine interpretation. We might even go onward, and pass into those ages which have become very bywords for perverted interpretation of Scripture—the ages of the earlier and later schoolmen—and even in them, amid subtile and narrow logic on this side, and a wild and speculative idealism on that, we should have no difficulty in showing that there was a *via media* of sound principles of interpretation which was both recognized and proceeded on. It is perfectly true that at this period not only the earlier threefold and fourfold senses of Scripture were re-asserted and re-applied, but that even sevenfold, eightfold,* and, if we choose to press the words of Erigena, infinite senses of Scripture were admitted by mediæval interpreters; but it is also perfectly true and demonstrable, from passing comments and cautions, that the simple, plain, and literal sense was always admitted to be the basis, and that other forms of interpretation were commonly regarded more in the light of deductions and applications. The rule laid down by Aquinas was clear enough, and expresses fairly the general feeling of the interpreters of his own time,—" In omnibus quæ Scriptura tradit, pro fundamento est tenenda veritas historica, et desuper spirituales expositiones fabricandæ" (*Summa Theol.* Pars. 1, Qu. 102, Art. 1): the literal and historical came first, the rest were forms of application. It is not, however, merely from passing comments, or from asserted, but really neglected principles, but from the general tenor of the better expositions of the time

* The enumeration may amuse the reader: (1) Sensus literalis vel historicus; (2) allegoricus vel parabolicus; (3) tropologicus vel etymologicus; (4) anagogicus vel analogicus; (5) typicus vel exemplaris; (6) anaphoricus vel proportionalis; (7) boarcademicus vel primordialis (*i.e.* quo ipsa principia rerum comparantur cum beatitudine æterna et tota dispensatione salutis); see *Bibl. Max. Patr.* tom. xvii. p. 315 seq. (Ludg. 1677.)

that the full force of the above remarks will best be felt. Let a fair and intelligent reader consent to give a little time to some of the interpretations of difficult passages in St. Paul's Epistles as put forward by Lombard or Aquinas, and then tell us his impressions. We will venture to state what his report would be,—that it was a matter of surprise to him, in an age which has ever been a very byword for subtilties and pedantry, to find such a large amount of reasonable and intelligent interpretation of the Word of God.

5. To gather up, then, our preceding comments, may we not fairly say,—*first*, that much that has been said about the extent and variety of interpretations of Scripture is exaggerated; *secondly*, that even the various methods of interpretation—which, when it serves a purpose, our opponents regard as meaning the same as the results arrived at—may in many, perhaps most, cases be regarded as modes of applying or expanding the primary sense, rather than of eliciting substantive and independent meanings; *thirdly*, not only that God has never left Himself without a witness, and that in every age there have been a few faithful representatives of faithful principles of interpretation, but further, that there has been from

the very earliest times, not only in theory but in practice, a plain, literal, and historical mode of interpreting Scripture ; and *finally*, that there may be traced so great an identity in the results arrived at by successive interpreters, that we have full warrant for using the term Catholic in reference to a far larger portion of what may be considered current orthodox interpretations than the mere popular disputant is at all aware of ? Let the inquire be put with all simplicity to those, whether in this country or abroad, who have made Ancient Versions and expositors their study, and, however different their opinions may be on other points, on this they will be agreed,—that there is such a *concordia discors* in the results obtained, that in very many passages we can produce interpretations which may stand even the test of Vincent of Lerins, and may justly be termed the traditional interpretations of the Church of Christ.

We know, of course, how these statements both have been and will be disposed of by the impatient and the confident. It will be said, probably, that granting merely for the sake of argument, that there is that species of concord of interpretation in many important passages, it has been only the result of traditional prejudices from which it is now our duty to make ourselves free. It will be added that any form of such consent is in itself suspicious, and that if our intuitions run counter to it we are at once to listen to the voice of reason within us, and reject the interpretation of every Church and every age of the world, if it does not approve itself to our own convictions. Brave and buoyant in our own self-esteem, we shall perhaps never pause to ask how far the so-called voice of reason may not be the voice of prejudice,—how far convictions may not be merely the results of secret influences within, and of some half-consciousness that what we reject bears aspects or involves conclusions sadly at variance with our habits or our propensions. We may at last perceive that it is the Word of God in its dreaded function of searching the intents of the heart that is now being brought home to us, and in our very dismay and perplexity we may have felt forced to come to the determination that every interpretation, be it of Church or of Council, that makes us thus tremble for ourselves, both must be and shall be either rejected or ignored. Thus, perhaps, will all that has been urged be disposed of. Be it so. There is a proud and confident spirit abroad ; there is a love of self,

self in its more purely intellectual aspects, above measure painful and revolting; there are forms bearing the names of moral goodness and freedom, and yet involving the denial of the essence of both, that bring an Apostle's predictions sadly and strangely to our thoughts,—and we feel it must be so, and that there are some whose ears must be and will be turned away from the truth. Yet there are others—especially the young, the ardent, the inexperienced—to whom what has been thus far urged may not have been urged in vain. To them our arguments are mainly addressed, to them we are speaking, for them we are pleading. "Young man, true in heart and earnest in spirit, honest searcher, anxious yet prayerful inquirer, let not thy eyes be holden by proud, unkindly hands, judge for thyself. Believe not every one that tells thee that the records of the Church are scribbled over with every form of strange, idle, and conventional interpretation of the Word of God. Judge for thyself, but judge righteous judgment. If there be fuller concords in the voices of the past than thou hast believed, close not thine ears to them because as yet they sound not fully harmonious to thee. Wait, ponder, pray: ere long, perchance thine own voice will spontaneously blend with what thou hearest; thou thyself, by the grace of God, may at length hear sounding round thee, and by thine own experience make others hear with thee, the holy accords and harmonies of the deep things of the Word of God."

§ 2.

6. We now pass naturally onward to another portion, or rather to another, and that at first sight an opposed, aspect of our present subject. Hitherto we have shown not only that the amount of the differences of interpretation has been clearly over-estimated, but even that the true and honest method of interpreting the Word of God—the literal, historical, and grammatical — has been recognized in every age, and that the results are to be seen in the agreement on numberless passages of importance that may be found in expositors of all periods; in other words, that the illuminating grace of God has ever been with His Church. This being so, it is but waste of time to consider the causes that have been alleged for the existence of the multitude of interpretations, when that multitude has been proved to a great extent to be imaginary. We will not, then,

pause to discuss the amount of varying interpretations that have been ascribed, whether, on the one hand, to rhetoric and desires to edify, or, on the other, to party feeling and efforts to wrest the meanings of Scripture to different sides. We deny not that both have produced some effect on the interpretation of Scripture. We do not deny that the Christian preacher may have often urged meanings that do not lie in the words, and that these may have been adopted by contemporaries and echoed and reproduced by those that have followed. We deny not, again, that the natural meaning of many texts may have been perverted by prejudice on one side or other, and that traces of this may still remain in some of the current interpretations of our own times. All this we deny not, but, on the other hand, we confidently assert that the effects have been limited, and that all the assumptions that the contrary has been the case fall with the fallen assumption, viz., that the discordance of Scripture interpretations is excessive, and that all methods hitherto adopted have been uncertain or untrustworthy

But we now come to what at first sight may appear a reversed aspect of our subject. While, on the one hand, we consider it proved that there has been from the first a substantial agreement, not only in the mode of interpreting Scripture, but in many of its most important details, we are equally prepared, on the other hand, to recognize the existence of great differences of opinion about the meanings of individual passages, and even in reference to the methods by which these meanings may be best obtained. No one who has had any experience in the interpretation of Scripture can with honesty assert the contrary. It may be true that in the great majority of all the more important passages careful consideration will show that what logic, grammar, and a proper valuation of the significance of words, seem to indicate as the principal and primary meaning of the passage, will be found to have been recognized as such ages before, and has substantially held its ground to our own times,—still experience teaches us that there is a very large residuum of less important passages in which interpreters break up into groups, and in which the expositor of the nineteenth century has to yield to the guidance of principles perhaps but recently recognized, yet, from their justice and truth, of an influence and authority that cannot be gainsaid. There are, indeed, even a few cases, but confessedly unimportant, where the modern interpreter has to oppose himself to every early Version and every patristic commentator, and where it is almost certain he is right in so doing. Let the connexion of the concluding portion of Gal. iv. 12 be cited as an example. Such instances are, however, very rare, and need hardly be mentioned save to show that principles can never be dispensed with, and that, though we yield all becoming deference to interpretations in which antiquity is mainly agreed, we yet by no means pledge ourselves unreservedly to accept them. All these differences, then, in the interpretations of individual passages, we frankly recognize ; nay more, we may in many cases admit that there are clearly defined differences in the method of interpreting—perhaps an extended context. Last of all, it is not to be supposed that there is a somewhat large class of passages so far-reaching, so inclusive, and so profound, that not only are all the better interpretations remarkable for their varied character, but for their appearing, perhaps each one, to represent a portion of the true meaning, but scarcely, all of them together, what our inner soul seems to tell us is the complete and ultimate meaning of the words that meet the outward eye.

7. We are thus admitting the existence of diversity of interpretation, especially in individual passages and details, as readily and as frankly as we have argued for the existence of a far greater prevailing unity both in the meanings themselves, and the methods of arriving at them in all more important passages, than is willingly recognized by popular writers. The question then naturally arises, how do we account for these apparently reversed aspects? How can we in the same breath assert prevailing unity, and yet admit diversity? How do we account for a state of things which in Sophocles or Plato would be pronounced incredible or absurd? Our answer is of a threefold nature. We account for this by observing, *First*, that the Bible is different to every other book in the world, and that its interpretation may well be supposed to involve many difficulties and diversities. *Secondly*, that the words of Scripture in many parts have more than one meaning and application. *Thirdly*, that Scripture is inspired, and that though written by man it is a revelation from God, and adumbrates His eternal plenitudes and perfections.

On each one of these forms of the answer we will make a few observations.

I. On the first, perhaps, little more need be said than has been incidentally brought forward in earlier parts of this Essay. It is, indeed, most unreasonable to compare, even in externals, the Bible with any other book in the world. A collection of many treatises, written in many different styles, and at many different ages, can never be put side by side with the works of a single author, nor will any canons of interpretation which may be just and reasonable in the latter case, be necessarily applicable to the former. What, for instance, can really be more strange than to lay down the rule that we are to interpret the Scripture like any other book, when, in the merest rough and outside view, the Scripture presents such striking differences from any book that the world has ever seen? The strangeness becomes greater when we look inward, and observe the varied nature of the contents,—prose and poetry, history and prophecy, teachings of an incarnate God, and exhortations and messages of men to men. How very unreasonable to insist on similar modes of interpreting what our very opponents rightly term " a world by itself "—a world from which foreign influences are to be excluded—and any other documents or records that have come from the hand of man! How can we with justice require that amount of exegetical agreement in the former case that might naturally be looked for and demanded in the latter? How very reasonable, on the other hand, is the supposition that in the interpretation of a collection of treatises of such varied and momentous import we may have to recognize both unities and diversities, —unities as due to the illuminating grace of the one and self-same Spirit similarly vouchsafed to all meek and holy readers of Scripture in every age of the Church,—diversities as due to the profundity and variety that must ever mark the outpourings of the manifold wisdom of God! It seems, indeed, idle to dwell upon what is thus obvious and self-evident ; but it has been rendered necessary by what we are obliged to term the unfairness of our opponents. At one time, when the argument seems to require it, the Scripture is considered as a single book, to be dealt with like other books, subject to the same critical canons, amenable to the same laws of interpretation: at another time it emerges to view as a collection of records, unconnected and discordant, which it is desirable to keep thus divided, that they may be the more readily disposed of ; and, whenever it may seem necessary, the more successfully pitted against one another in contradictions and antagonisms.

II. We pass onward to our second form of answer. Here we find ourselves, as might have been foreseen, in undisguised conflict with the sceptical writers of our own time. That Scripture has one meaning, and one meaning only, is their fundamental axiom: it is seen to be, and felt to be, one of the keys of their position. When, however, we pause to ask how that one meaning is to be defined, we receive answers that are neither very intelligible nor consistent. If we are told that it is "that meaning which it had to the mind of the Prophet or Evangelist who first uttered or wrote, to the hearers or readers who first received the message," we may justly protest against an answer involving alike such assumptions and such ambiguities. What right have we to assume that the speaker knew the full meaning which his own words might subsequently be found to bear? A very little reflection will show the justice of this query. What right, again, have we to assume that the meaning which the Prophet or Evangelist designed to convey was identical with that which the hearers or readers who first received the message conceived to be conveyed in its words? Assuming even that it was so, how are we to arrive at this one meaning common to hearer and speaker? How are we to recognize it, when the words before us may bear two or more meanings, each, perhaps, equally probable and supported by arguments of equal validity? It will be said that this is precisely the duty of the Interpreter; that it is for him to disengage himself from the trammels of the present, and free from the bondage of prejudices and creeds to transport himself back into the past, to mingle in spirit with those who first heard the words, to feel as they felt, to hear as they heard, to recover the one, the true, and the original meaning, and to bring it back to the hearer or reader of our own times. All this is high-sounding and rhetorical; it is sure to attract the young and the enthusiastic, and by no means ill-calculated to excite and delude the inexperienced. But it is rhetoric, and nothing more. No one who has had genuine experience in the interpretation of Scripture would hesitate to pronounce such " magnifyings of an office" as completely delusive, if even not deserving the graver term, mischievous. Delusive they certainly are, because all this self-projection into the past is in reality, and ever has been, unostentatiously practised by all better interpreters—by all who have sought with humility and earnestness to catch the spirit and mind of the writer whom they are striving to expound. All this has been practised, almost from the first. Chrysostom spoke of it, Augustine commended it, and yet what has been the result of experience? Why, that passage after passage has been found to be so pregnant with meaning, so mysteriously full, so comprehensively applicable, that the most self-confident interpreter in the world could scarcely be brought to declare his complete conviction that the one view out of many which he may have adopted was certainly the principal one, much less that it was the only meaning of the words before him.

But to give up such attitudes of delusive self-confidence, and to return to modesty and reason, we may now proceed to illustrate our first assertion, that Scripture has frequently more than one meaning, by references to three particulars in which this is very clearly exemplified,—double meanings, or applications of prophecy, types, and deeper senses of simple historical statements. A few remarks shall be made on each.

(1.) On the first so much has been said of late that it might almost seem pure knight-errantry to undertake the advocacy of what (we are told) ought now to be regarded as a mere outworn prejudice. And yet what is more thoroughly consonant with reason, and, we might almost add, experience, than such a belief? We say experience,—for there must be few calm observers of the course of events around them who can fail to have been struck with the curious re-appearance, under unlikely circumstances, of former combinations, and who have not occasionally been almost startled by the recurrence of incidents in relations and connexions that could never have been reasonably expected again. It does not seem too much to say that in many instances nations and individuals alike seem moving as it were in spirals, constantly returning, not exactly to the same point, but to the same bearings and the same aspects,—not precisely to a former past, but to a present that bears to it a very strange and wholly unlooked-for resemblance. If this be true in many things that fall under our own immediate observation (and very unobservant must he be who has not often verified it for himself), if we often seem to ourselves to recognize this principle of events becoming in many respects doubles of each other, and that not only in minor matters, but even in circumstances of some historical importance,—if this be so, is it strange that in the spiritual history of our race there should be such parallelisms; that words apparently spoken in reference to a precursory series of events should be found to refer with equal pertinence to some mysteriously similar combinations that appeared long afterwards? Are we to think that counsels sealed in silence from eternity, that purposes of the ages formed before the worlds were made, that dispensations of love and mercy laid out even before the objects for whom they were designed had come into being, were not over and over again reflected, as it were, in the history of our race, and that the events of a former day were not often bound in mystical likenesses and affinities with the events of the future by that principle of redeeming love which permeated and pervaded all? Unless we are prepared plainly to adopt some of the bleakest theories of the scepticism of these later days; unless we are determined to find civilization and development and not God in history; unless we have resolved to see in the Gospel no foreordered dispensation, but only a system of morality, unannounced, unforeshadowed, as strange in its isolated and exceptional character as it has been strange in its effects,—then, and then only, can we consistently deny the likelihood and probability of God's purposes to the world having imparted to events seemingly remote and unconnected, and to issues brought about by varied and dissimilar circumstances, real and spiritual resemblances. Then only can we justly deny that the word of prophecy might truly, legitimately, and consistently be considered to refer as well to earlier as to later events, wherever such resemblances could be reasonably demonstrated to exist.

To illustrate the foregoing comments by an example, let us take an instance which our opponents are never wearied with bringing forward,—our Lord's prophecy relative to the fate of Jerusalem and the end of the world. Here it is said that the system of first and second meanings, which we are now defending, is most palpably nothing whatever else than an attempt to help out the verification and mitigate the incoherence of a somewhat confused and partially unrealized prophecy. Now, in disposing of this idle but painfully familiar comment, we will make no allusion to the question of the four Apostles, which, it may be observed, necessitated in the answer reference to the end of the world as well as to the end of the Theocracy (Matt. xxiv. 3) ; we will only take the prophecy as we find it, with its mingled allusions to a near and to a remote future, and simply inquire whether there is any such resemblance, spiritual or otherwise, as might make expressions used in reference to the one almost interchangeably applicable to the other. Who can doubt what the answer must be? Who that takes into consideration the true significance of the fall of Jerusalem, who that sees in it, as every sober reader must see, not merely the fall of an ancient city, but the destruction of the visible seat of Jehovah's worship, the enforced cessation of the ancient order of things, the practical abrogation of the Theocracy,—all closely synchronous with the Lord's first coming,—who is there that will take all these things fairly into consideration and not be ready to acknowledge resemblances between the end of the fated city and the issues of the present dispensation, sufficiently mysterious and sufficiently profound to warrant our even alternating between them (we use the studiedly exaggerated language of opponents) the verses of the Lord's great prophecy? Till it can be shown that the course of things is fortuitous, that providential dispensations are a dream, and the gradual development of the counsels of God a convenient fiction—till it can be made clear to demonstration, that there are no profound harmonies in the Divine government, no mystical recurrences of foreordered combinations, no spiritual affinities between the past and the present, no foreseen resemblances in epochal events, and no predestined counterparts, the ground on which the reasonable belief in double meanings and double applications of prophecy has been rightly judged to rest will remain stable and unshaken; the perspective character that has been attributed to Scriptural predictions will still claim to be considered no idle or unreal imagination.

(2) The subject of *types* has been much dwelt upon by modern writers, and in most cases with unsingular fairness. The popular mode of arguing on this subject is to select some instances from early Christian writers which are obviously fanciful and untenable, to hold up the skirts of their folly, to display their utter nakedness, and then to ask if a system of which these are examples either can or ought to be regarded with any degree of favor or confidence. If Justin tells us that the king of Assyria signified Herod, and Jerome was of opinion that by Chaldæans are

meant Dæmons, if the scarlet thread of Rahab has been deemed to have a hidden meaning, and the number of Abraham's followers has been regarded as not wholly without significance, we are asked whether we can deem the whole system otherwise than precarious and extravagant, whether we can at all safely attribute to the details of the Mosaic ritual a reference to the New Testament, or really believe that the passage of the Red Sea can be very certainly considered a type of baptism. The ultimate design of this mode of arguing will not escape the intelligent reader ;—it is simply an endeavor by slow sap to weaken the authority of some of the writers of the New Testament, and to leave it to be inferred that our Lord Himself, in recognizing and even giving sanction to such applications of Scripture (Matt. xii. 40, John iii. 14 ; comp. ch. vi. 58), either condescended to adopt forms of illustration which he must have felt to be untrustworthy, or else really in this did not rise wholly above the culture of His own times. Now at present, without at all desiring to press what we have not yet discussed—the inspiration of Scripture—we do very earnestly call upon those who are not yet prepared wholly to fling off their allegiance to Scripture, to bear in mind the following facts :—(*a*) That our Blessed Lord Himself referred to the Brazen Serpent as typical of his being raised aloft, and that He illustrated the mystery of His own abode in the chambers of the earth by an event of the past which He Himself was pleased to denominate as a sign,—the only sign that was to be vouchsafed to the generation that then was seeking for one ; (*b*) that the Evangelists recognize the existence and significance of types in reference to our Lord (Matt. ii. 15 ; John xix. 36) ; (*c*) that the teaching of St. Paul is pervaded by references to this form of what has been termed "acted prophecies" (Rom. v. 14 *seq.*; 1 Cor. v. 7, x. 2 *seq.*; Gal. iv. 24 *seq.*; Col. ii. 11) ; (*d*) that the greater part of the Epistle to the Hebrews is one continued elucidation of the spiritual significance of the principal features of the Levitical law : its sacrifices, rites, and priests were all the shadows and typical resemblances of good things to come (Heb. x. 1) ; (*e*) that St. Peter plainly and distinctly declares that the water of the Flood is typical of baptism (1 Pet. iii. 21) : (*f*) that in the last and most mysterious revelation of God to man the very realms of blessedness and glory are designated by a name and specified by allusions (Rev. xxi. 22) which warrant our recognizing in the Holy City on earth, the "Jerusalem that now is," a type of that Heavenly City which God hath prepared for the faithful (Heb. xi. 16), a similitude of the Jerusalem that is above, a shadow of the incorruptible inheritance of the servants and children of God.

When we dwell calmly upon these things, when we observe further how, not only thus directly and explicitly, but how, also, indirectly and by allusion, nearly every writer in the New Testament bears witness to the existence and significance of types, how it tinges their language of consolation (Rev. xxi. 2 *seq.*), and gives force to their exhortations (Heb. iv. 14); when we finally note how the very Eternal Spirit of God, by whom they were inspired, is specially declared to have vouchsafed thus to involve in the ceremonies of the past the deep truths of the future (Heb. ix. 8), when we calmly consider the cumulative force of all these examples and all these testimonies, we may perhaps be induced to pause before we adopt the sweeping statements that have been made in reference to the whole system of typology. We may admit that types may have been often injudiciously applied, that it may be difficult to fix bounds to their use or to specify the measure of their aptitude, and yet we may indeed seriously ask for time to consider whether such recognitions of the deeper meanings of Scripture thus vouchsafed to us, and thus sanctioned by our Lord and His Apostles, are to be given up at once because they are thought to come in collision with modern views of Scripture and modern canons of interpretation. Our opponents may well be anxious to get rid of the whole system of types; we can understand their anxiety, we can even find reasons for the sort of desperation that scruples not to represent what was once sanctioned by our Lord and His Apostles as now either mischievous or inapplicable. It is felt that if typology is admitted, the assertion that Scripture has but one meaning is invalidated. It is seen clearly enough that if it can be shown, within any reasonable degree of probability, that the details of a past dispensation were regarded by the first teachers of Christianity as veritable types and symbols of things that have now come, then the recognition of further and deeper meanings in Scripture, of secondary senses and ultimate significations, must directly and inevitably follow, and the rule that the Bible is to be interpreted like any other book at once be shown to be, what it certainly is, inapplicable. Need we wonder then that every effort has been made to denounce a system so obstructive to modern innovations; need we be surprised that the rejection of what is thus accredited has been as persistent as it would now seem proved to be both unreasonable and without success?

(3.) Our third subject for consideration, the existence of deeper meanings in Scripture, even in what might seem simple historical statements, follows very naturally after what has just been discussed. Here again we can adopt no more convincing mode of demonstration than is supplied by an appeal to Scripture. Yet we may not unprofitably make one or two preliminary comments. In the first place, is not this assertion of a oneness of meaning in the written words of an intelligent author open to some discussion? Is it at all clear, even in the case of uninspired writers, that the primary and literal meaning is the only meaning which is to be recognized in their words? Is it so wholly inconceivable that more meanings than one may have been actually designed at the time of writing, and that, conjointly with a leading and primary meaning, a secondary and subordinate meaning may have been felt, recognized, and intended? Nay, can we be perfectly certain that even words may not have been specially or instinctively chose which should leave this secondary meaning fairly distinct and fairly recognizable? It would not be difficult to substantiate the justice of these queries by actual examples from the writings of any of the greater authors whether of our own or some other country. Still less difficult would it be to show that in very many passages meanings must certainly be admitted which it may be probable were not intended by the writer, but which nevertheless by their force and pertinence make it frequently doubtful whether what has been assumed to be the primary meaning of the words is really to be deemed so, and whether what is judged to be an application may not really represent the truest aspects of the mind and intentions of the author.

Let us add this second remark, that the instances in which words have been found to involve meanings, not recognized at the time by reader or by writer, but which after-circumstances have shown were really to be regarded as meanings, are by no means few or exceptional. The whole group of illustrations supplied by "ominata verba," the whole class of cases which belong to that sort of unconscious prescience which is often found in minds of higher strain, the various instances where glimpses of yet undiscovered relations have given a tinge to expressions which will only be fully understood and realized when those relations are themselves fully known,— all these things, and many more than these, might be adduced as illustrative of the deeper meanings that are often found to lie in the words of mere uninspired men. Such meanings neither they nor their own contemporaries may have distinctly recognized, but meanings they are notwithstanding; not merely applications or extensions, but meanings in the simple and regular acceptation of the term. How this is to be accounted for, we are not called upon to show. We will not speculate how far the great and the good of every age and nation may have been moved by the inworking Spirit of God to declare truths of wider application than they themselves may have felt or realized; we will not seek to estimate the varying degrees of that power of partially foreseeing future relations which long and patient study of the past and the present has sometimes been found to impart. All such things are probably beyond our grasp, and would most likely be found to elude our present powers and present means of appreciation. With reasons we will not embarrass ourselves; we will be satisfied with simply calling attention to the fact that the existence of such phenomena as that of words having deeper and fuller meanings than they were understood to have at first is not only not to be denied, but may even be deemed matter of something more than occasional experience.

The two foregoing observations will, perhaps, have in some measure prepared us for forming a more just estimate of the further and second meanings that have been attributed to the words of Scripture. If it be admitted that some of the phenomena to which we have alluded are occasionally to be recognized in purely human writings, is it altogether strange that in a revelation from God the same should exist in fuller measures, and under still clearer aspects? If the many-sidedness, mobility, and varied powers of combination existing in the human mind, appear at times to invest words written or spoken with a significance of a fuller and deeper kind than may at first be recognized, are we to be surprised if something similar in kind, but higher in degree, is to be observed in the language of Holy Scripture? Is the Divine mind not to have influences which are conceded to the human? Are the words of Prophets or Evangelists to be less pregnant in meaning, or more circumscribed in their applications, than those of poets and philosophers? Without assuming one attribute in the Scripture beyond what all our more reasonable opponents would be willing to concede, without claiming more for it than to be considered a revelaion from God, a communication from the Divine mind to the minds and hearts of men, we may justly claim some hearing for this form of the *à priori* argument; we may with reason ask all fair disputants whether they are prepared positively to deny, in the case of a communication directly or even indirectly from God, the probability of our finding there some enhancement of the higher characteristics and more remarkable phenomena that have been recognized in communications of man to men?

When we leave these *à priori* considerations, and turn to definite examples and illustrations, our anticipations cannot be said to have disappointed us. We have really an affluence of examples of second and deeper meanings being deliberately assigned to passages of Scripture that might have been otherwise deemed to have only the one simple or historical meaning that seems first to present itself. Let us select two or three instances. Is it possible to deny that our Lord Himself discloses, in what might have been deemed a mere title of Jehovah under His aspects of relation to favored worshippers, a meaning so full and so deep that it formed the basis of an argument (Matt. xxii. 31 *seq.* ; Mark xii. 24 *seq.* ; Luke xx. 37 *seq.*) ? The familiar titular designation is shown to be the vehicle of a spiritual truth of the widest application ; the apparently mere recapitulation of the names of a son, a father, and a grandfather, in connexion with the God whose servants they were, and whom they worshipped, is not only urged as proving a fundamental doctrine, but is tacitly acknowledged to have done so by gainsayers and opponents (Luke xx. 39). And further, let it be observed, that it is clearly implied that this was no deeply-hidden meaning, no profound interpretation, which it might require a special revelation to disclose, but that it was a meaning which really ought to have been recognized by a deeper reader,— at any rate that not to have done so argued as plain an ignorance of the Written Word as it did of the power and operations of God (Matt. xxii. 29). Let this really " prerogative" example be fairly considered and properly estimated, and then let it be asked if the existence of deeper meanings in Scripture can consistently be denied by any who profess a belief in our Lord Jesus Christ. It seems to us that this is a plain case of a dilemma: either with Strauss and Hase we must regard the argument as an example of Rabbinical sophistry,—and so, as Meyer reminds us, be prepared to sacrifice the character and dignity of our Lord,—or we must admit that, in some cases at least, there is more in Scripture than the mere literal sense of the words.

Such an example opens the way for the introduction of others, which without this prerogative instance, could not have been strongly urged, except on assumptions which, in our present position in the argument, it would not be logically consistent to make. By being associated, however, with the present example, they certainly seem to be of some force and validity in confirming our present assertion, and, to say the very least, can be more easily explained on that hypothesis than on any other that has yet been assigned. Let us specify Matt. ii. 15. Now the question presents itself in the following form:—Is not this an example furnished by the Apostle of what we have already seen must be recognized in an example vouchsafed by his Lord? Is not this a case of deeper meaning? Do not the words of Hosea, the second meaning of which was doubtless not more apparent even to the prophet himself than it was to his earlier readers, seem only to have a simple historical reference to the earthly Israel? and yet do they not really involve a further and typical reference to Him who was truly and essentially what Israel was graciously denominated (Exod. iv. 22; comp. Jerem. xxxi. 9), and of whom Israel was a type and a shadow? So, at any rate, St. Matthew plainly asserts. Which, then, of these hypotheses do we think most probable,—that St. Matthew erroneously ascribed a meaning to words which they do not and were not intended to bear, that the two chapters are an interpolation (for such an hypothesis has been advanced), or that they supply an instance of a second and typical meaning in words of a simply historical aspect, and that a truth is here disclosed by an Apostle similar to what we have already seen has been clearly disclosed by our Lord?

Let us take yet another, and that, as it might be thought, a very hopeless instance. St. Paul, in his Epistle to the Ephesians (ch. iv. 8), not only makes a citation from a Psalm, which at the part in question appears to have a simple historical reference to some event of the time (perhaps the taking of Rabbah), but even alters the words of the original so as to make its application to our Lord more pertinent and telling. What are we to say of such a case? Does it not really look like an instance of almost unwarrantable accommodation? Does it not seem as if we had now fairly fallen upon the point of our own sword, and that, in citing an example of a second meaning, we had unwittingly selected one in which the very alteration shows that the words did not originally have the meaning now attributed to them? Before we thus yield, let us at any rate state the case, and leave the fair reader to form his own opinion. Without at present assuming the existence of any influence which would have directly prevented the Apostle from so seriously misunderstanding and so gravely misapplying a passage of the Old Testament, and only assuming it as proved that there is one authentic instance of words of Scripture bearing a further meaning than meets the eye, we now ask which is to be judged as most likely: that the Apostle to substantiate a statement, which could have been easily substantiated by other passages, deliberately altered a portion of Scripture which had no reference to the matter before him, or that he rightly assigned to a seemingly historical passage from a Psalm, which (be it observed), in its original scope, has every appearance of being prophetic and Messianic, a deeper meaning than the words seem to bear (such a meaning being in one case, at least, admitted to exist), and that he altered the form of the words to make more palpable and evident the meaning which he knew they involved? We have no anxiety as to the decision in the case of any calm-judging and unbiassed reader. . . . . . One further remark we may make in conclusion, and it is a remark of some little importance, viz., that if the present instance be deemed an example of Scripture having a second and deeper, as well as a first and more simple meaning, it must also be regarded as an example of an authoritative change in the exact words of a quotation,—the change being designed to bring up the underlying meaning which was known to exist, and to place it with more distinctness before the mind of the general reader.

III. Having thus, as it would seem, substantiated our assertion that deeper meanings lie in Scripture than appear on the surface, and that this may be properly considered as in part accounting for the existence of some of those difficulties and diversities which are met with in Scripture interpretation, we now pass to the third assertion relative to the subject, viz., that Scripture is *divinely inspired.*

Here we enter upon a wide subject, which may with reason claim for itself a separate and independent essay, and which certainly ought fully to be disposed of before any rules bearing upon interpretation can properly be laid down. As a longer discussion of this subject will be found in another portion of our volume, we will here only make a very few general remarks upon inspiration as immediately bearing upon interpretation, and more especially upon the estimate formed of its nature and extent by the advocates of the system of Scriptural exegesis now under our consideration.

In the outset, let it be said that we heartily concur with the majority of our opponents in rejecting all theories of inspiration, and in sweeping aside all those distinctions and definitions which, only in too many cases, have been merely called forth by emergencies, and drawn up for no other purpose than to meet real and supposed difficulties. The remark probably is just, that most of the current explanations err more especially in attempting to define what, though real, is incapable of being defined in an exact manner. Hence all such iterms as "mechanical" and "dynamical" inspiration, and all the theories that have grown round these epithets,—all such distinctions as inspirations of superintendence, inspirations of suggestion, and so forth,—all attempts again to draw lines of demarcation between the inspiration of the books of Scripture themselves and the inspiration of the authors of which those books were results, may be most profitably dismissed from our thoughts, and the whole subject calmly reconsidered from what may be termed a Scriptural point of view. The holy Volume itself shall explain to us the nature of that influence by which it is pervaded and quickened.

8. Thus far we are perfectly in accord with our opponents. We are agreed on both sides that there *is* such a thing as inspiration in reference to the Scriptures, and we are further agreed that the Scriptures themselves are the best sources of information on the subject. Here, however, all agreement completely ceases. When we invite our opponents to go with us to the Scriptures to discuss their state-

ments on the subject before us, and to compare the inferences and deductions that either side may make from them, we at once find that by an appeal to Scripture we and our opponents mean something utterly and entirely different. *We* mean a consideration of what Scripture says about itself: we find that *they* mean a stock-taking of its errors and inaccuracies, of its antagonisms with science and its oppositions to history,—all which they tell us must first be estimated, and with all which they urge, that inspiration, be it whatever it may, must be reconcilable and harmonized. In a word, both sides have started from the first on widely different assumptions. *We* assume that what Scripture says is trustworthy, and so conceive that it may be fittingly appealed to as a witness concerning its own characteristics; *they* assume that it abounds in errors and incongruities, and suggest that the number and nature of these ought to be generally ascertained before any further step can be taken, or any opinion safely arrived at on the whole subject. Such seems a fair estimate of the position and attitude of the two contending parties.

If this statement of our relative positions be just, it seems perfectly clear that several different lines of argument may be adopted. We may examine the grounds on which their assumption rests, or endeavor to establish the validity of our own. We may deny that any errors or inaccuracies exist, and throw upon them the *onus probandi*, or we may take the most popular and telling instances in their enumeration and endeavor to discover by fair investigation how far they deserve their position, and how far prejudice and exaggeration may not have been at work on their side, as conservatism and accommodation on ours. All these are courses which may be adopted with more or less advantage, but any one of which would occupy far more space than we can afford for this portion of our subject. We must satisfy ourselves, on the present occasion, with making, on the one hand, a few affirmative comments upon the nature, degree, and limits of the inspiration which we assign to the Scripture; and on the other hand, a few negative comments upon counter-statements advanced by opponents, which seem more than usually untrustworthy.

To begin with the negative side, let us observe, in the first place, that nothing can really be less tenable than the assertion that there is no foundation in the Gospels or Epistles for any of the higher or supernatural views of inspiration. It is a perfectly intelligible line of argument to assert that for the testimony of any book upon its own nature and characteristics to be worth anything, it must first be shown that the book can fully be relied on: it is quite consistent with fair reasoning to refuse to accept as final or conclusive the evidence of what it may be contended has been shown to be a damaged witness. Such modes of argument are quite fair and intelligible, and as such we have no fault to find with them; but to make at the outset an assertion, such as we are now considering,—to prejudice the minds of the inexperienced by an affirmation, which, if believed, cannot fail to produce the strongest possible effect, and which all the time is the very reverse of what is the fact, is indeed very like that "random scattering of uneasiness" which has been attributed to our opponents,* and which such cases as the present go very far to substantiate. It is scarcely possible that those who make such assertions can be ignorant of the terms in which our Lord is represented by the Gospels to have spoken about the Scriptures of the Old Testament.

* See Moberly, Preface to 'Sermons on the Beatitudes,' p. ii.

It cannot surely be forgotten that He said that they "could not be broken" (John x. 35), and that when He so spake He was using Scripture in a manner that almost vouched for its verbal and literal infallibility. It cannot have been overlooked that when He was citing the words of David He defined the divine influence under which those words were uttered (Mark xii. 36). Does not an Evangelist record His promise to His Apostles that the Holy Ghost "should teach them all things, and bring all things which He said to them to their remembrance" (John xiv. 26)? and does not that same Evangelist mention the yet more inclusive promise that the same Eternal Spirit should lead the Disciples into "the whole truth" (John xvi. 13)? and are such words to be explained away or to be limited? Does not the same writer further tell us that the Holy Ghost was almost visibly given to the Apostles by the Lord Himself (John xx. 22)? and does not another Evangelist tell of the completed fulness of that gift, and of men so visibly filled with the Holy Spirit that the lips of bystanders and strangers bore their ready and amazed testimony? Have we no foundation for asserting a higher inspiration when eleven men are told by a parting Lord that they are to be His witnesses, and that they are to receive supernatural assistance for their mission? Is testimony to be confined to words spoken, and to be denied to words written? Did the power that glowed in the heart of the speaker die out when he took up the pen of the writer? Was not, again, the "demonstration of the Spirit" laid claim to by St. Paul (1 Cor. ii. 4); was it not "God's wisdom" that he spake (ver. 7)? Does he not plainly say that the things "which God prepared for those that love Him," His purposes of mercy and counsels of love, were revealed to him by God through the agency of the Spirit (ver. 10)? and does he not enhance his declaration not only by affirmatively stating from whom his teaching was directly imparted, but by stating, on the negative side, that to man's wisdom he owed it not? Yea, and lest it should be thought that such high prerogatives belonged only to words spoken by the lips, does not the same Apostle guard himself, as it were, by claiming for his written words an origin equally Divine? and does he not make the recognition of this a very test of illumination and spirituality (1 Cor. xiv. 37). We pause, not from lack of further statements, but from the feeling that quite enough has been said to lead any fair reader to pronounce the assertion of there being " no foundation" in the Gospels or Epistles for any of the higher or supernatural views of inspiration contrary to evidence, and perhaps even to admit that such assertions, where ignorance cannot be pleaded in extenuation, are not to be deemed consistent with fair and creditable argument. To deny the worth or validity of such testimony is perfectly compatible with fair controversy ; to deny its existence in the teeth of such evidence,—and such evidence is known and patent,—can only be designed to give a bias to a reader, and to raise up antecedent prejudices in reference to subjects and opinions afterwards to be introduced. How far such a mode of dealing with grave questions is just or defensible, we will leave others to decide.

Let us make a second remark of a somewhat similar character, and earnestly protest against hazy and indefinite modes of speaking about the testimony of the Church in reference to the doctrine of inspiration. Whether the Church is right or wrong in its estimate of the nature and limits of this gift, is certainly a question which those who feel the necessity of inquiry are perfectly at liberty to entertain. We may pity a state of mind that is not moved

SCRIPTURE: ITS INTERPRETATION. 149

by such authority, and we may suspect it to be ill-balanced; but we do not complain of such a mode of proceeding. If a man wishes to find out whether the Early Church, for instance, is right or wrong in its estimate of a principle or a doctrine, let him (in a serious and anxious spirit) commence his investigation, but let him not seek by vague and indefinite language to make it first doubtful whether the Early Church really did form any estimate at all,— when that estimate is plainly set down in black and white in fifty different treatises. Let us, at any rate, have a clear understanding on the question at issue, and agree as honest men to throw no doubts upon simple matters of simplest fact. Now, when we are told that the term inspiration is but of yesterday, and more especially that the question of inspiration was not determined by Fathers of the Church, we do seem justified in protesting against such really unfair attempts to gain over those who have neither the time, the knowledge, nor perhaps the will, to test the truth of the assertion. Let there be no mistake on this subject. The Fathers of the Church may be right or they may be wrong; but, at any rate, on this topic they have spoken most frequently and most plainly, and if any question in the world may be considered determined by them this certainly is one. The Apostolical Fathers term the Scriptures "the true sayings" of the Holy Ghost (Clem. Rom. *ad Cor.* i. 45). In quoting passages from the Old Testament they often use the significant formula "the Holy Ghost saith." Those that followed them used their language. Justin Martyr describes the nature of inspiration, and even hints at its limits (*Cohort.* § 8); Irenæus speaks of the Scriptures as "spoken by the Word of God and His Spirit" (*Hær.* ii. 28. 2); and even attributes to the foresight of the Eternal Spirit the choice of this rather than that mode of expression in the opening words of St. Matthew's Gospel (*Hær.* iii. 16. 2). In quoting a prophet, Clement of Alexandria pauses to correct himself, and say it was not so much the prophet as the Holy Spirit in him (*Cohort.* § 8, p. 66), and on the question of Scripture infallibility and perfection he is no less precise and definite (*Cohort.* § 9, p. 68; *Strom.* ii. p. 432, vii. p. 897, ed. Potter). Tertullian and Cyprian carry onward the common sentiment; those who follow them reiterate the same so frequently and so definitively that we become embarrassed by the very affluence of our examples. Eusebius of Cæsarea deals even with technicalities, and brands those who dared to say that the writers of Scripture put one name in the place of another (*Comment. in Psalm.* xxxiii., ed. Montf.). Augustine states most explicitly his views on the whole subject, and asserts the infallibility of Scripture in language which the strongest asserter of the so-called bibliolatry of the day could not desire to see made more definite or unqualified (see for example *Epist.* lxxxii. 3, *tom.* ii. p. 285, ed. Bened. 2). . . . Again we pause. We could continue such quotations almost indefinitely. We could put our fingers positively on hundreds of such passages in the writings of the Fathers of the first five or six centuries; we could quote the language of early Councils; we could point to the silent testimony of early controversies, each side claiming Scripture to be that from which there could be no appeal; we could even call in heretics, and prove from their own defences of their own tenets, from their own admissions and their own assumptions, that the inspiration of Scripture was of all subjects one that was conceived thoroughly settled and agreed upon. Enough, however, has perhaps been said, enough quoted, to place the matter beyond doubt, and to make this perfectly certain,—that what are called high views of inspiration were entertained almost unanimously by the earlier writers of the Church. So obvious, indeed, is the fact that writers like Gfrörer not only concede the fact of the agreement of the early writers, and admit the strong opinions they held on the subject, but use it as a very ground of reproach against them, and call upon us to wonder how men who entertained such high views on the inspiration of Scripture could possibly be such arbitrary and unfaithful interpreters.

A third remark may be made on the negative side by way of complaint that we find so little weight assigned to the subjective argument, as it may be termed, for the inspiration of Scripture. In the sceptical writings of the day the argument is rarely stated except to be dealt with as a form of a natural but not very harmless illusion. Yet it is an argument of the greatest force and importance, and an argument which, if rightly handled, it is much easier to set aside than to answer. Is it nothing that the Bible has spoken to millions upon millions of hearts, as it were with the very voice of God Himself? Have not its words burned within till men have seen palpably the Divine in that which spake to them? Is it not a fact that convictions on the nature of the Scriptures deepen with deepening study of them? Ask the simple man to whom the Bible has long become the daily friend and counsellor, who reads and applies what he reads as far as his natural powers enable him; ask him whether longer and more continued study has altered to any extent his estimate of the Book as a Divine revelation. What is the invariable answer? The Book "has found him;" it has consoled him in sorrows for which there seemed no consolation on this side the grave; it has wiped away tears that it seemed could only be wiped away in that far land where sadness shall be no more; it has pleaded gently during long seasons of spiritual coldness; it has infused strength in hours of weakness; it has calmed in moments of excitement; it has given to better emotions a permanence, and to stirred-up feelings a reality; it has made itself felt to be what it is; out of the abundance of his heart the mouth speaks, and he tells us with all the accumulated convictions of an honest mind, that if he once deemed the Bible to be fully inspired on the testimony of others, now he knows it on evidence that has been brought home to his own soul. He has now long had the witness in himself, and that witness he feels and knows is unchangeably and enduringly true.

Ask, again, the professed student of Scripture, the scholar, the divine, the interpreter, one who, to what we may term the testimony of the soul, in the case of the less cultivated reader, can add the testimony of the mind and the spirit,—ask such a one whether increased familiarity with Scripture has quickened or obscured his perception of the Divine within it, whether it has led him to higher or to lower views of inspiration. Have not, we may perhaps anxiously ask, the difficulties of Scripture wearied him, its seeming discordances perplexed, its obscurities depressed him? Have not the tenor of its arguments, and the seeming want of coherence and connexion in adjacent sentences, sometimes awakened uneasy and disquieting thoughts? What is almost invariably the answer?—"No; far otherwise." Deepened study has brought its blessing and its balm. It has shown how what might seem the greatest difficulties often turn merely upon our ignorance of one or two unrecorded facts or relations; it has conducted to standing-points where in a moment all that has hitherto seemed confused and distorted has arranged itself in truest symmetry and in the fairest perspective. In many an obscure passage our student will tell us how the light has ofttimes suddenly broken, how he has been cheered by being permitted to recognize and identify the commingling of human weakness and Divine power, the mighty revelation almost too great for mortal utterance, the " earthen vessel " almost parting asunder from the greatness and abundance of the heavenly treasure committed to it. He will tell us, again, how in many a portion where the logical connexion has seemed suspended or doubtful,—in one of those discourses, for instance, of his Lord as recorded by St. John,—the true connexion has at length slowly and mysteriously disclosed itself, how he has perceived and realized all. For a while he has felt himself thinking as his Saviour vouchsafed to think, in part beholding truth as those Divine eyes beheld it ; for a brief space his mind has seemed to be consciously one with the mind of Christ. All this he has perceived and felt. And he will tell us, perchance, what has often been the sequel ; how he has risen from his desk and fallen on his knees, and with uplifted voice blessed and adored Almighty God for His gift of the Book of Life.

The cold-hearted may smile at such things.

the so-called philosophical may affect to account for them ; they may be put aside as illusions, or they may be explained away as projections of self on the passive page, unconscious infusion of one's own feelings and emotions in the calm words that meet the outward eye. All this has been urged against such testimony, and will ever be urged even to the very end. But when the end does come the truth will appear. That witnessing of soul and spirit will, it may be, rise up in silent judgment against many a one who now slights it ; that testimony so often rejected as self-engendered and fanciful, will be seen to have been real and heaven-born, a reflex image of an eternal truth, a part and a portion of the surest of the sure things of God.

9. But let us now pass from the negative to the positive, and make a few affirmative observations on the subject before us. Let us begin, not with a theory, but with a definition and a statement of the belief that is in us. If asked to define what we mean by the inspiration of Scripture, let us be bold, and make answer—that fully convinced as we are that the Scripture is the revelation through human media of the infinite mind of God to the finite mind of man, and recognizing as we do both a human

and a Divine element in the written Word, we verily believe that the Holy Ghost was so breathed into the mind of the writer, so illumined his spirit and pervaded his thoughts, that, while nothing that individualized him as man was taken away, everything that was necessary to enable him to declare Divine Truth in all its fulness was bestowed and superadded. And, as consonant with this, we further believe that this influence of the Spirit, whether by illumination, suggestion, superintendence, or all combined, extended itself—*first*, to the enunciation of sentiments and doctrines, that so the will and counsels of God should not be a matter of doubt, but of certain knowledge; *secondly*, to statements, recitals, facts, that so the truth into which the writer was led should be known and recognized; *thirdly*, to the choice of expressions, modes of speech, and perhaps occasionally even of words (the individuality of the writer being conserved), that so the subject-matter of the revelation might be conveyed in the fittest and most appropriate language, and in the garb best calculated to set off its dignity and commend its truth.

Let such be our definition. If asked how we justify it, how we prove our assertions, we answer in two ways: first, by *à priori* arguments of great force and validity; secondly, by *à posteriori* arguments of equal or even greater strength—arguments which our preceding remarks on the negative side have been designed indirectly to set forward and substantiate. Into these arguments we do not intend to enter, but we may profitably pause to specify them. On the *à priori* side, and especially in reference to the Old Testament, we may specify evidences of inspiration derived from the clear accordance of various events with prophecies special or general that can be proved to have been uttered before the events in question. Among instances of this nature the history and present state of the Jews have been always rightly and confidently appealed to.* Again, on the same side, but more in reference to the New Testament, it has been fairly urged that, if we admit the general truth and Divine character of the Christian dispensation, we can hardly believe that those who were chosen to declare its principles and to make known its doctrines were not especially guarded from error in the execution of their weighty commission, and were

* See Moberly, Preface to 'Sermons on the Beatitudes,' p. xxxii.

not divinely guided both in the words they uttered and the statements they committed to writing. On the *à posteriori* side we may specify the three great arguments to which we have already alluded : the direct declarations of Scripture, the trustworthy character of Scripture having been first demonstrated ;* the unanimous consent of the early writers, and unchanging testimony of the Catholic Church ; and, lastly, the inward and subjective testimony to the Divine nature of the Scripture yielded by the soul and spirit of the individual. Other arguments there are, especially on the *à priori* side, of varying degrees of strength and solidity, appealing in different ways to different minds ; but the chief perhaps have been specified, and on these we may safely and securely base our preceding assertions, and our unhesitating and unqualified belief in the full inspiration of the Word of God.

But it may be asked, how do we conceive that this inspiration took place ? What is our

* Thus to appeal to Scripture to define its own character in reference to inspiration seems perfectly fair, when the trustworthy character of the volume has been properly demonstrated ; compare the remarks of Chalmers, 'Christian Evidences,' iv. 2. 26, vol. iv., p. 390. (Glasgow ed.)

theory of the process? what do we conceive to be the *modus agendi* of the Holy Spirit in the heart of man? This we plainly refuse to answer. We know not, and do not presume to inquire into the manner; we recognize and believe in the fact. Individual writers may have speculated; imagery, suitable or unsuitable, may have been introduced as illustrative by a few thinkers in early ages; but the Catholic Church has never put forward a theory. On this subject she has always maintained a solemn reserve; she declares to us that in the Scripture the Holy Ghost speaks to us by the mouths of men; she permits us to recognize a Divine and a human element; but, in reference to the nature, extent, and special circumstances of the union, she warns us not to seek to be wise above what has been written, not to endanger our faith with speculations and conjectures about that which has not been revealed. Theories of inspiration are what scepticism is ever craving for; it is the voice of hapless unbelief that is ever loudest in its call for explanation of the manner of the assumed union of the Divine with the human, or of the proportions in which each element is to be admitted and recognized. Such explanations have not been vouchsafed, and it is as vain and unbecoming to demand them as it is to require a theory of the union of the Divinity and Humanity in the person of Christ, or an estimate of the proportions in which the two perfect natures are to be conceived to co-exist.

Not much more profitable is the inquiry into the exact limits of inspiration, whether it is to be considered in all cases as extending to words, or whether it is only to be confined to sentiments and doctrines. At first sight we might be inclined to adopt the latter statement, and such, to some extent, would certainly seem to have been the view of a writer of no less antiquity and learning than Justin Martyr; still when we remember, on the one hand, that there are instances in Scripture in which weighty arguments have in some degree been seen to depend on the very words and expressions that are made use of (John x. 34; Gal. iii. 16), and on the other, that many important truths must have lost much of their force and significance if they had not been expressed exactly with that verbal precision which the subject-matter might have demanded, we shall be wise either to forbear coming to any decision, or else to adopt that guarded view which we have already indirectly advocated, viz., that in all passages of importance, wheresoever the natural powers of the writer would not have supplied the befitting word or expression, there it was supplied by the real though probably unperceived influence of the Spirit of God.

A question of far greater moment, and far more practical importance, is that which relates to the exact degree of the inspiration, the fallibility or infallibility of the Sacred Records. Was the inspiration such as wholly to preclude errors and inaccuracies, or was it such as can be compatible with either one or the other? This is clearly the real anxious question of our own times, and one to which we must briefly return an answer, as general canons of interpretation must obviously to some extent be modified by the opinions we form on a subject which so seriously affects the character of the documents before us. Let us pause for a moment to consider the answer that is now commonly returned by those among us who claim be considered of advanced thought and intelligence. They tell us, in language of unrestrained confidence, that no man of candor can fail to acknowledge the existence not only of mistakes as to matters of minor importance, but of such positive " patches of human passion and error," such " weakness of memory," or such "mingling of it with imagination," such "feebleness of inference, such confusion of illustration with argument," and such variations in judgment and opinion, that in the study of Scripture we must continually have recourse to a "rectifying or verifying faculty," that we may properly be enabled to separate the Divine from the human,—what is true, real, and unprejudiced, from what is perverted, mistaken, and false. In a word, the Sacred writers now stand charged with errors of two kinds,—errors of mind and judgment, and errors in matters of fact, but on evidence (as the following remarks will tend to show) which cannot be regarded either as sufficient or conclusive.

To substantiate the first class of errors we may commonly observe two modes of proceeding: on the one hand, the more reckless method of citing difficult texts, assuming that they contain a meaning arbitrarily fixed on by the critic, and probably not intended by the writer, and then censuring him for not having intelligibly expressed it; on the other hand, the more guarded but equally mischievous suggestion that the logic of the Scriptures is *rhetorical* in character, and that such passages as Rom. i. 16 *seq.*, Rom. iii. 19, al., are examples of some forms of error in reasoning, and such oppositions as "light and darkness," "good and evil," "the Spirit and the flesh," "the sheep and the goats," oppositions of ideas only, which are not realized in fact and experience. With regard to these methods, we will say briefly that the first is unfair and discreditable ; the second, simple assertion that can either be disproved in detail, or that fairly admits of counter-assertion of greater probable truth.

The second class of alleged errors is, at first sight, of more importance and plausibility. It professes to include oppositions to science, oppositions to received history, and cases of direct mutual contradiction. Of these three forms we may again briefly say that instances of the first kind, far from increasing, are steadily decreasing under a just comparison of the true meaning of the words of Scripture with the accredited conclusions of science. Recent discussions of the subjects of controversy by men of acknowledged scientific attainments have tended to show that the oppositions of Scripture and science are really far more doubtful than they are assumed to be, and that though they still hold a very prominent place on the pages of the charlatan, they one by one disappear from the treatises of men of real science who have scholarship sufficient to extract the real meaning of the language of Scripture in the passages under consideration. . . . Much the same sort of remark, *mutatis mutandis*, may be made on alleged oppositions to received History or Chronology; many of the supposed oppositions held in former times to be inexplicable have now entirely passed away from the scene, and have alike ceased to stimulate the sceptic or to disquiet the believer; others, like the case of Cyrenius (Luke ii. 2), are all but gone; and as to what remain there is a growing feeling among unbiassed scholars and historians that if we could but obtain the knowledge of a few more facts relative to the various points at issue, the oppositions of Scripture and History would wholly cease to exist. . . . In regard of mutual contradictions, it might be thought a better case has been made out. Writers from whom we might have looked for more guarded comment have done much to exaggerate the so-called discrepancies of the Scripture narrative, and have somewhat too emphatically denounced modes of explanation that, both from their simplicity and, not unfrequently, their antiquity, have very great claims on our consideration. Sceptics have not been slow to take advantage of this ill-advised course. When, however, all these so-called contradictions are mustered up, they are but a motley and an enfeebled host. We survey them, and we observe some as old as the days of Celsus, and as decrepit as they are old; others vainly hiding all but mortal wounds received in conflicts of the past, and now only craving a *coup de grace* from some combatant of our own times; some of a later date, and a more aspiring air, recruited from Deistical controversies of a century or two back, but all marked with uncomely scars, and armed with nothing better than broken or corroded weapons. There they stand; the discrepancy between two Evangelists about the original dwelling-place of Mary and Joseph, explained and well explained fourteen hundred years ago; the two genealogies, fairly discussed in ancient times, and in our own explained in a manner that approaches to positive demonstration; the blasphemy of the *two* thieves, disposed of very reasonably by Chrysostom, and since his time on the same or a similar principle by every unprejudiced commentator; the narrative of the woman who anointed our Lord's feet, first prepared for the occasion by the assumption that the narratives in all the four Gospels relate to the *same* woman,—an assumption regarded even by Meyer, and apparently De Wette, as plainly contrary to the fact. And so on. When we survey such a company, and are told that, at any rate, we should respect their numbers, their aggregate authority, their cumulative weight, an uneasy feeling arises in the mind that those who parade them must really be aware that there is something amiss with each case, that, however numerically strong they may be, it is disagreeably true that as individual instances they are disabled or weak. If so, is there not a great responsibility resting on those who bring forward catalogues of such instances, and yet do not apprise the simple and the inexperienced that each supposed difficulty has most certainly been met over and over again, and with very reasonable success; that this array, so to be respected for its numbers, is really strong in nothing else,—a mere rabble of half-armed or disarmed men?

But finally, it may be said, are we prepared to assert that no inaccuracy, even in what all might agree in regarding as a wholly unimportant matter of fact,—a date, for instance, or a name, or a popular statement of an indifferent matter,—either has been, or can ever be, found in the whole compass of Scripture? To that question, in its categorical form, we should perhaps be wise in refusing positively to return any answer. We have no theory of inspiration, we only state what we find to be a matter of fact, we only put forward what those facts and the testimony of the Church alike warrant us in defining as the true and Catholic doctrine. We have no means of settling definitely whether a *posse peccare* in minor matters may, or may not, be compatible with a Divine revelation communicated through human media; but certainly till inaccuracies, fairly and incontestably proved to be so, are brought home to the Scripture, we seem logically justified in believing that as it is with nine-tenths of the alleged contradictions in Scripture, so is it with the alleged inaccuracy. Either the so-called inaccuracy is due to our ignorance of some simple fact, which, if known, would explain all; or it is really only an illustration of one of those very conditions and characteristics of human testimony, however honest and truthful, without which it would cease to be human testimony at all. If positively forced to state our opinion, we will express what we believe to be the true doctrine of inspiration in this particular by an example and a simile. As in the case of the Incarnate Word we fully recognize in the Lord's humanity all essentially human limitations and weaknesses, the hunger, the thirst, and the weariness on the side of the body, and the gradual development on the side of the human mind (Luke ii. 40),—in a word, all that belongs to the essential and original characteristics of the pure form of the nature He vouchsafed to assume, but plainly deny the existence therein of the faintest trace of sin, or of moral or mental imperfection,—even so in the case of the written Word, viewed on its purely human side, *and in its reference to matters previously admitted to have no bearing on Divine truth*, we may admit therein the existence of such incompleteness, such limitations, and such imperfections as belong even to the highest forms of purely truthful *human* testimony, but consistently deny the existence of mistaken views, perversion, misrepresentation, and any form whatever of consciously committed error or inaccuracy.

10. We have thus at length touched upon all the main points in which the doctrine of the inspiration of Scripture is in any degree likely to come in contact with rules and principles of interpretation. Less than this could

not have been said. Less it was not logically consistent to say. It may, indeed, seem plausible to urge that we have no right to express any prior opinion on such subject; that we have only to apply to Scripture the ordinary rules of interpretation which we observe in the case of other books, and that we ought to leave the question of inspiration to be settled by the results we arrive at. Is it not, however, abundantly clear that if there be even a low presumption, arising from external or internal evidence, for supposing that the Scripture *has* characteristics which render it very unlike any other book, then it is only right and reasonable to examine that evidence before we apply rules of interpretation which, perhaps, may be found in the sequel to be inadmissible or inapplicable? Surely, on the very face of the matter it seems somewhat strange to be told to interpret the Scripture like any other book, while in the same breath it is avowed that there are many respects in which Scripture is unlike any other book. It is really very much the same as being told to ascertain with a two-foot rule the precise linear dimensions of a room of which it is known or admitted that the sides are not always straight, but variously curved and embayed. The application of our two-foot rule would doubtless put very clearly before us, if we had ever doubted it, not only the fact that bays and curvatures really did exist, but also that the instrument in our hands was a singularly unfit one for measuring what it was plain required something less rigid and impracticable. The duty of the two-foot rule would really then be over, unless we chose to reserve it for those parts where the walls somewhat more nearly conformed to the straight line. If, however, we desired properly to complete our task, we should have to go home for our measuring-tape.

www.ingramcontent.com/pod-product-compliance
Lightning Source LLC
Chambersburg PA
CBHW022116160426
43197CB00009B/1048